Play it Again

Chris Horrie

Play it Again

Discover your musical abilities

Collins

First published in 2007 by
Collins, an imprint of
HarperCollins Publishers
77-85 Fulham Palace Road
Hammersmith, London W6 8JB

www.collins.co.uk

11 10 09 08 07
6 5 4 3 2 1

A catalogue record for this book is available from the British Library.

Main photography by Mark Read
Celebrity photography by Craig Hacker (Frank Skinner), Alex Maguire (Diane Abbott, Aled Jones, Bill Oddie, Robert Winston), Stuart Wood (Jo Brand)
Edited by Emma Callery
Designed by Jon Hill
Illustrations by Kat Heyes

ISBN: 978-0-00-725036-3

Colour reproduction by Dot Gradations Ltd, UK.
Printed and bound in Great Britain by Butler and Tanner.

Contents

Introduction

Each year, millions of children start to learn to a play a musical instrument. Sadly, most will give up, often leaving them with a sense of failure that cuts them off from the world of music making for good. That's a tragedy. The philosophy behind *Play it Again* is that nobody ever loses their natural musical ability, and anyone can return to music making at any point in their later lives.

To prove the point, the *Play it Again* team asked six celebrities with very different backgrounds and personalities to either learn how to play a musical instrument of their choice from scratch, or to learn to play their 'dream instrument', the one they might have chosen for themselves, rather than the one they were sometimes reluctantly directed to in their schooldays.

Professor Robert Winston, for example, had not touched any sort of instrument since playing the primary school recorder. But he was able to turn his deep love for classical music into an ability to play the saxophone, in just a couple of months. **Jo Brand** had been a competent piano player as a schoolgirl. But she had been put off playing the instrument as part of rebelling against her past. She returned to performance by playing the church pipe organ – much more dramatic and fun. **Aled Jones** started out as a choirboy. Partly to shake off that image and explore another musical world, he took to playing drums in a heavy metal rock group. Politician **Diane Abbott**, on the other hand, was learning piano for the first time. **Bill Oddie** always knew he had musical talent, but had never got round to having formal lessons, even though he was not completely convinced that he needed them in order to master the electric guitar. **Frank Skinner** took to the banjo – the ultimate outlaw instrument – just because he wanted to play something unusual and different.

This book guides you through the process of learning a musical instrument, from the first decision about what type of music and instrument you want to play to tips on performance and joining a group of fellow enthusiasts.

As the TV series shows, it may be difficult to start playing again after years of inactivity. But so long as you make the right choice of instrument and move at the pace that's right for you, there are huge benefits ranging from improved memory and concentration to better health and a more varied social life.

Learning to play an instrument is an increasingly popular activity with adults. It is fun, rewarding, relaxing – and much easier than most people think. So what are you waiting for?

Chapter 1

Why play music?

It is in us all

At the simplest level, music is the combination of two things: beat and melody. The appeal of the beat is universal. It may well evoke memories of being in the womb, of the regular and comforting throb of the heart. Scientists have found that music with a beat close to the resting state of an adult woman – between 70 and 80 beats per minute (bpm) – causes the brain to produce calming alpha waves. This, in turn, promotes relaxation, the ability to concentrate and feelings of wellbeing. Faster music causes alarm and excitement. Is it because a faster beating heart usually means trouble – having to run away from danger, for example?

A great deal of music – pop, jazz or classical – is played at a beat just a little faster than the resting heart rate, matching a condition where the body is awake, slightly stimulated but still resting.

'Wisdom is not truth. Truth is not beauty. Beauty is not love. Love is not music. Music is THE BEST...'

FRANK ZAPPA, GUITARIST

- Any music with a beat of 100 bpm or over is thought of as 'fast'.
- Very speedy house, techno and dance music uses beats of up to180 bpm – more than double the resting heart rate of an adult male.
- A style of electronic music called speed core uses beats of 200 bpm. It would be dangerous even for a trained athlete to dance in time to speed core for more than a couple of minutes.

Beat also enables us to add structure to time. Just think of the ticking of a clock – it is through regular beats that we measure out our lives and make sense of the world. Musicians use special clocks called metronomes to measure beat. Indeed, music itself has been described as 'sculpture made from time'. It is easy to take beat and its appeal for granted. But if you stop to think about it, life itself begins and ends with a single beat of the heart. Every living thing beats.

People today are far more familiar with beat and structured time than in any previous generation. You can't get away from it. Clocks and timing devices are everywhere. Electronics has even enabled us to hear the beat of the heart itself (amplified with 5,000 watts of power, as at a rock concert) – an impossible achievement before the 20th century.

Zildjian
5B
Zildjian
5B

Pop music naturally emphasises beat over melody, because beat crosses barriers of age and culture much more easily than melody, or tunefulness. What sounds melodic in one culture may seem like a hideous din, at first, to somebody from another. But beat is universal. If you are aiming to be understood and appreciated by the largest number of listeners, then the beat has to be up front – it is immediately understood by people of all ages, in all cultures.

If you are thinking of learning a musical instrument, or reviving an interest in playing one, mastering beat is half the battle. And if you have grown up in a modern society, you will have been immersed in beat all your life, receiving a fantastic free musical education in the background without even noticing it.

Melodic musings

Just as the attraction of beat derives in some way from the heartbeat, scientists and musicologists believe that the attraction of melody is closely related to patterns of speech. Check this out with a simple experiment. Hum the famous opening 'Da-da-da-dahhh' theme from Beethoven's Fifth Symphony. Now sing the phrases, 'I've hurt my thumb' and, for the second bit, 'you've hurt yours too' to the same tune.

> 'I realised by using the high notes of the chords as a melodic line, and by the right harmonic progression, I could play what I heard inside me. That's when I was born.'
>
> CHARLIE PARKER, JAZZ SAXOPHONIST

This was not always the theory, however. In the second half of the 18th century, when Mozart was composing, the belief was that melody pre-existed in some heavenly and eternal sphere that individuals with special gifts, such as Mozart himself, were capable of hearing and passing on to mere mortals.

But according to today's thinking, Mozart's listeners liked what they heard not because it was the voice of ideal perfection, but because they were listening to their own speech patterns (and those of their parents, friends and lovers) being played back to them in a sublime form and with a perfectly judged matching beat.

For many years, contemporary composers have been explicitly using human speech patterns to create melody. Composers like Steve Reich, Philip Glass and John Adams have written mesmeric and highly melodic works based on replaying taped snippets of human speech over and over. In some types of modern pop music – especially rap – the melody consists only of speech patterns, put together with a heavy beat to produce music. And parents will have been charmed by the 'jargoning' phase that infants go through when developing the ability to speak.

Music, then, consists of beat and melody – the two things written down in musical notation. But it might be more useful to say it is a combination of banging and humming, or a perfect union of heart and mind.

It increases brain power

In recent years, neurologists have developed something of an obsession with using music as a way of exploring the way the brain works. As a result, there is a growing body of evidence showing that music plays a crucial role in developing parts of the brain used for processing language. A few years ago, for example, 'The Mozart Effect' – the idea that babies who listen to classical music in the womb turn out to be more intelligent than those who do not – was widely reported in the press. The theory is controversial, though it does have its scientific supporters, as discussed on page 16.

There is growing support, however, for the idea that the processes both of singing and of making music of any type – rather than just listening to it – has a wide range of benefits for the brain.

Developing brain size

In 2005, scientists Patrick Bermudez and Robert Zatorre told a conference in Germany that the right brain cortex of people who regularly played a musical instrument tended to be significantly larger than those of non-musicians.

The finding was based on MRI scans of the brains of large numbers of musicians and non-musicians. The biggest difference, they said, was likely to be found in subjects who had been playing music since they were very young. But the same effect was present in all the musical brains, regardless of the age at which their owner took up their instrument. The enlargement was noted, as might be expected, only in the parts of the cortex used for processing sound.

Increasing brain power

Other scientists claim that music playing might increase overall brain power because it simultaneously exercises areas of the brain dealing with spatial reasoning, language processing and, generally, the ability to listen very carefully for slight differences in sound. In other words, playing music is a great mind workout because of the way it fine-tunes the processing power of the brain.

Until the 1990s, it was widely thought that people who had not learned a musical instrument by the age of about 11 had little chance of taking one up

The Mozart effect

In 1993, scientists Francis Rauscher and Gordon Shaw claimed that ten minutes spent listening to a Mozart sonata improved the ability of university students to solve certain types of mental problems. Their work became popularly known as 'The Mozart Effect' – the idea that children, in particular, could become more intelligent just by listening to works by Wolfgang Amadeus.

The students had been asked to fold up a piece of paper and then cut shapes out of the folds with scissors. They then had to accurately predict what the shapes would look like when the paper was unfolded – which is quite tricky. It turned out that students who had listened to Mozart's music performed this arcane task more accurately than those who had not.

The scientists explaining that the positive effect applied only to 'spatial reasoning' (tracking shapes through changes in angle and direction) and, anyway, lasted only for 10–15 minutes. They never claimed that Mozart could improve brain power overall. The research, however, caused a sensation and was widely reported all around the world as a 'brain miracle'.

Later work by researchers in the same field found that the same effect could be achieved by getting subjects to concentrate on any piece of music before being handed the scissors. Since they had used tunes by the rock band Blur, they re-christened the results The Blur Effect.

in later life. It was thought that the music neurons 'stopped growing' and if they were not fully conditioned in very early life, they never would be.

More recent studies have shown this to be untrue. People taking up instruments, even after their 60th birthday, will experience new life in the specifically musical parts of their brain. This fact has been demonstrated – and celebrated – with the formation of the New Horizons Band set up in 1991 by Dr Roy Ernst at Eastman School of Music in Rochester, New York. The band was formed from adults aged between 50 and 85 years of age, most of who had never played an instrument before. The band was such a huge success that over a hundred New Horizons Bands have been set up in towns and cities across the USA and there are plans to spread the movement around the world – see www.newhorizonsmusic.org/nhima.htm.

Developing other skills

Scientist Sebastian Jentschke has shown that musically trained people are generally much better at learning languages, reacting much more strongly at the physical level to the discordant sound patterns in wrongly spoken words and sentences.

Other scientists have claimed that memorising music in order to play it can help in the process of maintaining memory function in old age, and in restoring memory function in patients with brain damage. The effect is achieved because the act of recalling a piece of music from the memory requires the brain cells to work together in a more synchronised way, building, retaining or restoring stronger neural pathways.

> 'Musically trained people are generally much better at learning languages.'
>
> SEBASTIAN JENTSCHKE, SCIENTIST

A study from the Netherlands has shown that people who regularly play music are far better at accurately imagining and then predicting the sound of various objects and situations that they are not actually hearing in real life, or may have never heard at all. The strong link between imagination of any sort – even audiovisual 'imaging', like this – and the capacity for intelligence is well known. ❚

You can make friends

Most instruments can be played either solo or as part of a group. Most amateur musicians will want to play for their own entertainment, at least to begin with, but joining a group, or playing alongside a friend or two, brings a whole range of additional pleasures, experiences and benefits.

The value of the internet

Through the internet you can instantly share your new interest in learning an instrument with thousands of others all around the world. The search term 'guitar resources' returns over 60 million sites, just in English. These sites deal with everything from basic, sensible lessons for beginners, through chat rooms and discussion groups, fan sites analysing the technique of particular players, free sheet music and cheap equipment, to step-by-step guides to making your own instrument and even wiring up your own amplifier.

The web-based piano community is just as large online, with considerable involvement from the world's great music schools, such as the Royal College of Music in London and the Julliard School in New York. These institutions offer invaluable advice. Online piano lessons, making use of the multimedia sound facilities now available on even the most basic laptop or home PC, are improving in quality. Some are free, and more are becoming available from a variety of amateur, commercial and academic suppliers (see page 147).

> 'Rock is so much fun. That's what it's all about – filling up the chest cavities and empty kneecaps and elbows.'
>
> JIMI HENDRIX, GUITARIST

Beyond the most popular instruments, there are perhaps more interesting – or at least colourful – web communities and sub-cultures devoted to instruments like the clavichord, accordion and the theremin – a weird electronic box that is played by moving the hands near two metal antennae to affect pitch and volume. You may have heard it the start of the Beach Boys' 'Good Vibrations', or on the soundtrack of any Sixties' sci-fi B-movie shocker. It is now very big in Japan. You can find out how to make one (surprisingly cheaply

and easily) on one enthusiast's site on the web at www.thereminplanet.com, and listen to rants of disgruntled players campaigning for the inclusion of the instrument in regular orchestras and chamber ensembles. Guaranteed to break the ice at parties.

Enjoying a cultural experience

If you are looking for a wider cultural experience, then you might be best advised to take up a folk or classical instrument.

The Irish and Scottish folk scene is huge in the UK and involves not only music performance but dance, storytelling and the study and discussion of history, culture and even politics. Likewise, the amateur classical music-making scene in the UK is said to be the best in the world, with orchestras and chamber groups of all sizes playing in most major towns in the country.

The bagpipes may be one of the ultimate challenges for the home-based musician (what will the neighbours think?), but it is a relatively easy instrument to play. Of course, as the hundreds of bagpipe enthusiast sites on the web indicate, the bagpipes in themselves constitute an entire branch of music. Most countries around the world, from China to Senegal, seem to have developed some sort of bagpipe-like instrument at some point in history. All of them are available to play – and your decision to attempt to do so would doubtless warm the cockles of a fellow bagpipe true believer somewhere in the world.

Each folk style from every country and region in the world has a presence on the web, as do many local amateur orchestras. In the UK, especially in the big cities, we are blessed with dozens of performing traditions. Joining a group interested in Celtic, Asian, Middle Eastern, Jewish or African folk music is an excellent way to reconnect with your roots – or to learn about another culture.

Cultural heritage and *Play it Again*

A part of Robert Winston's motivation in picking the saxophone is the central role the instrument plays in Jewish musical culture. For him, it is part of getting back to his roots and – however well or badly he ends up being able to play – understanding a little more about the way in which the music he is interested in exploring is made.

The same is true of Frank Skinner. In his case, the choice of banjo is partly about connecting with the traditions of music hall and popular entertainers.

Jo Brand's efforts to play the organ not only revives her interest in Gothic horror, it connects her to a tradition in literature and music and to the history of the church. It could open the door to all manner of intellectual interests.

An international language

The great thing about music is that it is a completely international language, and players form an international community. World music is ever more popular, and there are folk traditions from Africa and Asia waiting to be explored by a more general UK population. A decision to master an African instrument like the marimba, finger harp, talking drum or cora (a west African lute made from a gourd), would open up the way to exploring (or reconnecting with) world music.

In the past decade, the film music of Bollywood and Punjabi folk and pop music in the form of Banghara has started to cross into the mainstream, just as reggae from the West Indies did the decades before that. It is much easier now to obtain Indian and Pakistani Banghara instruments like the dholak and tumbi, or to learn to play the harmonium or flute in a traditional Indian or Pakistani style.

There is also a tradition of Islamic Sufi instrument playing, which has so far remained largely confined to the British Muslim community. A lot of it involves vocal chanting aimed at clearing the mind and controlling breathing. This is the music of trance dancers, 'whirling dervishes' and snake charmers.

Sufi works as a combination of music making and a type of yoga, and involves the whole mind and body. It may also be the historic root, spreading from the Muslim world to America via West Africa, of the hypnotic heavy beat of gospel, jazz and, ultimately, rock and pop music. Sufi music, which can also be performed on adapted versions of Western instruments (especially the voice-like reed instruments), is the great undiscovered gem of British music making.

> 'Music is one of the closest link-ups with God that we can probably experience. I think it's a common vibrating tone of the musical notes that holds all life together.'
>
> MARVIN GAYE, SINGER AND SONGWRITER

For something more traditional, the website Forming Bands at www.formingbands.co.uk puts together players of rock and jazz band instruments in seconds. You simply enter your address and the instrument you play (or are learning to play), and offers ranging from gigs to practice and jam sessions are made by return of e-mail. It works like a massive, continuous, online musical dating site.

It has health benefits

Whatever instrument you play – or are thinking of taking up – remember that there are associated physical and mental challenges. If you want to build up your muscle tone in your arms, play the flute or double bass; for lung control, take up the oboe or bassoon. The most onerous instrument of all time is thought to have been the bombarde – a huge bass woodwind instrument used in French Breton folk music. Playing one of those would have been a bit of a challenge.

Music-making aids relaxation

A 2005 scientific study found that people who play a musical instrument have a reduced risk of heart disease. According to the study, people who play music regularly, as opposed to just listening to it, control their breathing so well that there is a marked reduction of strain on the heart and lungs. Further, the musician's great feeling for beat and tempo leads to a greater ability to relax, especially when playing, and reduces stress in the body generally.

The lead researcher, Professor Peter Sleight, told journalists that 'appropriate selection of music, alternating fast and slower rhythms and pauses, can be used to induce relaxation, and so can potentially be useful for cardiovascular disease.'

In 2005, scientists at a US medical school found that the protein that translates sound waves in the ear into nerve signals is the same one that creates the perception of pain. Thus, when we hear a very loud or threatening sound, it creates extreme anxiety because of a pain-like reaction in the brain. Conversely, a perception of silence also causes anxiety. It was therefore found that the pain reaction is neutralised by familiar and lightly modulated sounds, such as

Claimed instrumental health benefits

- String instruments, especially the harp, have been shown to relieve chronic pain in cancer patients
- Female singing can reduce dangerously high heart rates in premature babies
- Drumming can stimulate the lymphatic system, boosting the body's immunity against disease

humming, which actually reduces pain in oneself and in others. Likewise, gentle music (like a gorgeous sweeping orchestral string arrangement) mimics the humming of a human's voice and sends the pain reaction into reverse.

It is this pleasure principle that experts and music advocates link to a range of life-enhancing health and social benefits that can be traced to performing music. Freed from the competitive pressures of the education system, and taken up as a voluntary pleasure, the process of learning to play a musical instrument can become a deeply relaxing and satisfying hobby.

Memory development

In the field of clinical music therapy, doctors have also discovered that memorising pieces of music for performance, even without learning to read music, can be used to maintain and help restore memory after episodes of brain damage.

What is driving the research into music and mental wellbeing is a series of striking discoveries made in the US in the 1990s, which show that listening to and performing music greatly speeds up the recovery of patients who suffer serious physical damage to the brain. It was found in study after study that music stimulated the brain overall and, in particular, 'exercised' those parts of it that dealt with memory and language.

It banishes the blues

The tremendous emotional power of music is amplified when you play it – or play along with it – instead of merely listening. And in the last few years there has been a flood of evidence about the huge positive impact on mental health that musical activity can have.

We shouldn't be surprised about this. After all, one of the major musical genres of modern times is 'the blues' – a literal and personal way of overcoming deep depression on the part of those anonymous folk geniuses who first played the music as a form of personal pain relief. Scientists have noted this antidepressive effect in several studies, and research is taking place into the exact way in which it works.

> 'One good thing about music, when it hits you, you feel no pain.'
>
> BOB MARLEY, REGGAE MUSICIAN AND SINGER

Learning to understand and play music, says psychologist Professor Susan Hallam of the University of London Institute of Education, helps concentration, aids relaxation and can influence moods and emotions: 'It can calm or arouse and help overcome anger, despair and other powerful emotions.' She adds: 'Music can help older people avoid feelings of loneliness and serve as a source of support for troubled teenagers. Singing in groups enhances the immune system, and there are lower mortality rates in people who attend cultural events or make music.'

'I really envy people who at a party can just sit at the piano and people call out songs and they can play it.'

 Bill Oddie plays the electric guitar

Bill Oddie plays the electric guitar

Bill Oddie is known to millions as the face of popular birdwatching and nature TV shows. He is also an accomplished stage performer and was one of the stars of *The Goodies*, a groundbreaking and much-loved Seventies comedy series.

Bill was born in Rochdale, just north of Manchester, and grew up in Birmingham. He was the only child of a very musical mother, who spent much of his childhood in hospital suffering from mental illness. There was not much music in the family home. Bill's earliest musical memories are all about the dreary sentimental songs that passed for pop music in those days. However, everything changed with the arrival of rock and roll at the end of the 1950s. Bill was hooked, spent all his pocket money on rock and roll records and formed a skiffle group with schoolmates.

Bill never had a guitar – or any sort of proper instrument. Instead, he played the washboard – a framed corrugated sheet originally used for scrubbing clothes, but pressed into service as the ultimate skiffle percussion instrument. Bill's job was to flail his fingers against the washboard, while his schoolmate Ivan played a double bass made out of a tea chest, a broom handle and a piece of string.

LEFT
I think, therefore I jam. Bill Oddie contemplates the world's most popular instrument.

The skiffle group didn't go anywhere. But Bill did. He was brilliant at school and made it to Pembroke College, Cambridge where, in the 1960s, he became part of the Cambridge Footlights, the comedy and theatrical group. The Footlights was going through a golden age – most of the *Monty Python* team was there at the same time – and for Bill it was the fast track to a career in national television. He became a performer and writer of spoof and satirical songs for a variety of cutting-edge radio and TV shows.

Bill's comedy career reached a peak in the Seventies with *The Goodies* – a hit TV series that worked as a surreal cross between a sketch show and a sitcom. Bill co-wrote and performed the show with Graeme Garden and Tim Brooke-Taylor. His on-stage role was that of the bearded, long-haired hippy nonconformist radical student protest activist.

As well as a TV show, The Goodies functioned as a pop group and in the mid-Seventies they had a string of hits including 'Father Christmas Do Not Touch Me', 'Black Pudding Bertha' and Bill's biggest hit – 'Do The Funky Gibbon'. Bill had no formal musical training, could not play an instrument and performed by clowning around and miming to tracks laid down by professional musicians.

Bill's musical journey

When Bill took up the *Play it Again* challenge he was making another series of wildlife programmes for the BBC. While extremely busy, he was also extremely enthusiastic. A deadline was looming – his highly musical daughter (who plays in a rock group) was about to have her 21st birthday. Bill wanted to learn the electric guitar, becoming good enough to play along with her live ... at least for one night.

As an aspiring guitarist, Bill has an important advantage – he has a very good 'ear' for music. The advantage may be partly genetic but it may also have been honed by bird-watching. For many people, the song of one bird will sound much like that of any other, but Bill has trained himself to recognise minute differences between the song of one type of a bird or another. He also has the advantage of his decades of composing and performing songs and musical routines and he is extremely knowledgeable about music – especially his favourite folk rock and blues music. He was, for a time, a DJ on Jazz FM in London.

For the purposes of *Play it Again*, Bill agreed to work with a teacher – the guitar expert and tutor Bridget Mermikides – though he maintained from the start that he might progress more quickly by teaching himself – if only he could muster the self-discipline needed for practice. Bill was also going to have a least one masterclass with Mark Knopfler and with other established rock and blues guitarists.

Bridget knew from the start that Bill was thinking about learning the instrument without her help. But she advised against that. 'It's always, always better to learn classical method first,' she said: 'Then there's a deep understanding and schooling that's in place.' Guitarists trained in the classical method are 'almost always better' when they take up the electric guitar.

Bridget set Bill the task of playing the old Bob Dylan standard 'Knockin' On Heaven's Door'. This meant learning how to play just three chords accurately and clearly. Once Bill had these three chords under his belt it would become much easier to learn others. The idea was to add more songs, one after the other, steadily increasing the number of chord progressions available to him.

During an early lesson, Bridget asked Bill to start practising the major chords of C, A, G, E and D – easy to remember because they spell out the word 'caged'. If Bill learnt these, and practised the permutations of changes between them, he would find himself able to play hundreds of songs. But Bill's natural musical abilities and performing skills meant that he wanted to move much more quickly than was ideal. Instead of putting in the hours, making sure the limited range of chord changes he had been set to learn

RIGHT
The electric guitar is a group instrument – perfect for socialising.

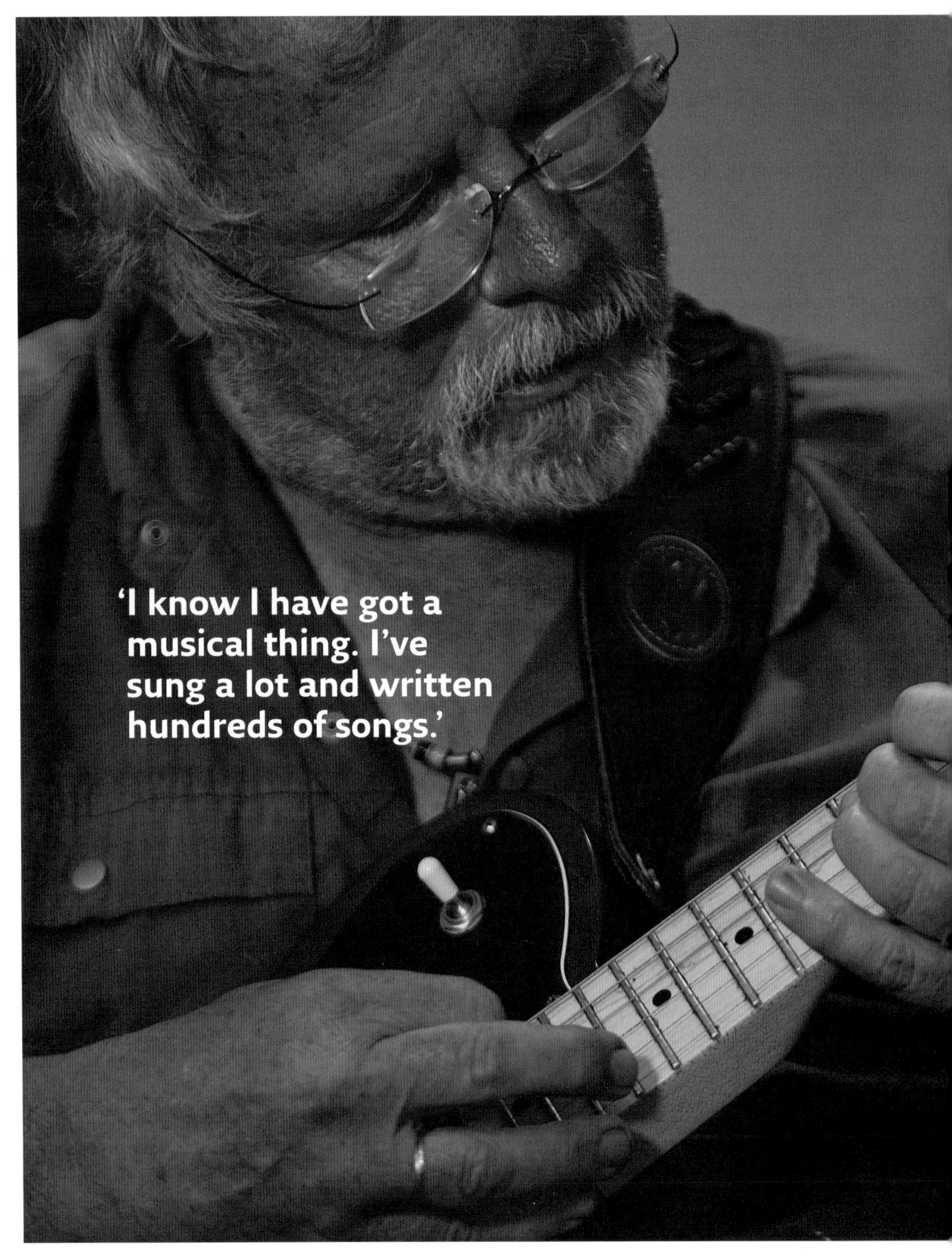

 Bill Oddie plays the electric guitar

became second nature, he wanted to race ahead, covering more ground – but more thinly.

The pressure was on. Bridget had arranged a public performance for Bill in just six weeks time, at the International Guitar Festival in Bath. She now changed tack. She still wanted Bill to learn the basics, but she allowed him to move on to the more immediately satisfying and creative activity of playing solos and lead guitar melody lines.

LEFT
The electric guitar is the perfect instrument for improvisation. Learning styles vary, and can be quite informal.

In two intensive days in a hired recording studio in the Royal Academy of Music, Bill immersed himself in practice and learnt how to play the most basic five-note pentatonic scale: C, D, E, G and A (the same notes as the chords he was initially asked to learn). This is a particularly useful tool because the notes in the scale will always harmonise with chords played in the same key on another instrument – no matter in what order they are played. Bill found it relatively easy to master the scale and within hours he was able to play short 'runs' or 'riffs' using the scale. With Bridget playing the chords to 'Knockin' On Heaven's Door', Bill, to his great delight, was able to extemporise in tune.

But on his second day in the studio, Bill had a session with the band he was going to perform with in Bath. A separate mike was set up to record each instrument so Bill couldn't hide behind the other musicians. The results weren't good and Bill hurried off at the end of the session, with Bridget knowing there would be no time for any further lessons or rehearsals before Bath.

Going public

After two weeks away filming in America, Bill – nervous and jet-lagged – had to walk straight into his performance at the festival in front of an audience of very discerning guitar fans. His showmanship and singing brought him through it, but Bridget was disappointed, feeling he still hadn't got the basic technique right.

Thinking afterwards about his performance at Bath, and his progress, Bill made a decision – he was going to teach himself. You did not necessarily need to practise technique in order to be a rock and roll guitarist. It was more about attitude, creativity, improvisation and performance.

In rock or blues, a messy 'raw' sound was much more appropriate then the polished, clean sound Bridget was aiming for. There was even a danger, Bill thought, that the creativity might be curbed by too much systematic practice.

Bill abandoned formal lessons and instead spent time with Dave Davies, lead guitarist with The Kinks and author of the legendary guitar riff 'You Really Got Me'. He was delighted to have his theories confirmed by Dave, who told him that the Kinks used to slash the cones of their amplifiers with knives to produce a distorted buzz-saw electric guitar sound. Bill was in his element 'thrashing' with the guitar, in typical hard rock – even punk rock – style. Effectively, he was using the guitar as a sort of electronic percussion instrument. A huge amount of sound – and rhythm – was produced by the way the string were struck, but there wasn't much there in the way of melody.

Bill also spent time with legendary electric guitarist Mark Knopfler, who achieved global fame with Dire Straits. He was very surprised to learn that Mark hadn't taken the route of endless lessons and practice which Bill had expected – a further confirmation of Bill's theory.

RIGHT
Sound investment: Bill enjoys a quiet moment alone with his guitar.

So, five months after he started, Bill had found a way to have fun with the electric guitar. It was similar to the way he thrashed around on the drum kit he kept at home for when he wanted to relax by having a great time making a lot of noise. But would it help him in his ambition with playing in his daughter's rock group at the party to celebrate her 21st birthday?

Rosie had been watching her dad's progress with interest – and amusement – throughout the whole *Play it Again* project. She recognised at the beginning how he was skipping all the basics and moving on to things more complicated than he was actually capable of playing. After his sessions with Mark Knopfler she was more positive. 'He has played obsessively, compulsively large amounts', she said. 'He's doing really well, much better than he was, definitely.'

The final challenge

While practising with Rosie's group for the big night, Bill adapted his performance-led style, changing from straight rock to a funky style. The number they were performing, and which Rosie was to sing, was very special. Rosie wrote 'Peaches and Cream' at the age of sixteen – a song about friendship and love, it had become a kind of family anthem. Bill was to accompany her, with the help of a bass guitarist, drummer and second, rhythm guitar, and the number would allow him to improvise around familiar chord patterns, C, D and G.

At a trendy London nightclub, Rosie's party was a huge event, with over a thousand guests. And just after midnight, Bill achieved his dream – he may not have played completely clean chords or the pentatonic scale, but with Rosie and her band he gave a great performance with a wonderful funky rhythm of his own. With some of the basics in place, and above all a determination to do things *his* way, he was starting to play the guitar the way he had always wanted. 'I've no idea whether it's okay, or terrible, or reasonably good,' he said, 'but what I do know is it gives me a great deal of satisfaction to do that.'

Chapter 2

Are you musical?

How good is your hearing?

Before committing the time and effort needed to learn an instrument, it might be worth checking the state of your hearing. Several companies selling hearing aids offer free, basic hearing tests. One such company, based in the United States, is called Free Hearing Test and is available online at www.freehearingtest.com/test.shtml. The site simply plays a series of tones using frequencies in the main speech range (half to eight kilohertz), with the tones that are most important for hearing clear speech being around the middle, between one and three kilohertz.

In the test, all the tones should appear to be about as loud as each other. If the lowest or highest tones sound fainter, you may have problems differentiating between the very high or low tones outside the normal speech range that are produced by some musical instruments.

Finding out more

To establish just how good your hearing is, you can go one step further by getting an audiogram produced – a sort of individual contour map of your hearing, tracing the peaks and valleys of your ability to hear high and low, or loud and soft notes.

Each person's audiogram is different and if you are worried, you should have it done by an ear and hearing specialist. But for a more light-hearted approach, you can create your own audiogram using an online hearing tests, such as that offered by the University of New South Wales at www.phys.unsw.edu.au/~jw/hearing.html. In a normal adult, the audiogram is flat in the middle – in the area between one and four kilohertz – showing that all the tones of normal human speech can be heard equally well. The line falls off smoothly for the highest and lowest frequencies, showing they are harder to hear (the higher the pitch, the higher the frequency). Younger children tend to be able to hear much higher pitches than adults.

An ability to hear notes outside the normal range or, more importantly, a better than average ability to perceive very quiet sounds at all frequencies, probably gives you an advantage in music because of a greater ability to distinguish clearly between the sounds of speech syllables and musical notes. If, on the other hand, the audiogram shows less hearing ability in a particular range, then it might be wise to avoid learning an instrument that uses that particular tonal range.

Do you have perfect pitch?

Alongside the physical abilities detected by an audiogram there is the question of pitch sensitivity – the ability to discriminate between different notes, to remember them and reproduce them accurately at will.

A person with 'perfect pitch' is able to sing accurately a given note from long-term memory without having it played to him or her first. Likewise, a person with perfect pitch is able to tell if an instrument is out of tune just by listening to a single note played on it. Having perfect pitch is strongly associated with the idea of the natural 'musical genius' and, especially, that of the child prodigy. Mozart had perfect pitch from birth. So did Beethoven. Many other great composers, however, including Wagner, Haydn, Brahms and Tchaikovsky, did not. Even after he became deaf, Beethoven retained his perfect pitch and was able to know exactly what a piece of written piece of music would sound like.

Perfect pitch is often described as a 'mystery' by psychologists. But it is now known to be closely associated with autistic spectrum disorders, where powers of memory are greatly exaggerated. It has also been found that while people with an ordinary ('relative') sense of pitch can identify and reproduce between 10 and 12 separate notes in an octave (the eight notes of the scale and a few 'slide' notes in between), people with perfect pitch can hear over seventy.

Or are you tone deaf?

The opposite end of the spectrum to perfect pitch is so-called 'tone deafness' – an inability to detect differences in sound or to hear a stream of music or sound as separate, identifiable notes. People who are tone deaf simply cannot remember what tunes are supposed to sound like and therefore cannot sing in tune or even in time. Just as perfect pitch is similar to the sort of phenomenal memory associated with autism, genuine tone deafness is similar to short- and long-term memory problems. Tone deafness is a sort of musical amnesia.

But many people with perfectly normal tone perception think they are 'tone deaf', which is perhaps just down to a lack of confidence in their abilities. In other words, they can sing or play a tune, but only when they have already heard it a few times and are familiar with it. The tentative sound of people singing an unfamiliar hymn in church, for example, is not tone deafness, it is mere unfamiliarity with the tune. All those bum notes result from people trying to guess where the melody might be going next, and getting it wrong.

Or are you somewhere in between?

The fact is that both these conditions – that of being tone deaf or of having perfect pitch – are extremely rare. According to research from University College London, up to 20 per cent of the population believe themselves to be tone deaf. The real incidence is less than one per cent.

You can test yourself online for true tone deafness at a website operated by the US National Institute for the Deaf at www.nidcd.nih.gov/tunetest/. The website works by playing 12 well-known tunes twice over at the click of a button. Sometimes the tune has been distorted and sometimes not. You are then asked if you heard any difference and you are given an instant automated response. As with the hearing tests, this online version should only be taken as a very rough guide. If you think you have a problem, contact a hearing specialist.

When it comes to perfect pitch, the estimates of how many people have the ability vary widely. Older research suggests that the ability is very rare, usually quoted as occurring naturally in only about one in 10,000 people. At the same time, it has been found that some ethnic groups – especially Chinese, Korean and Japanese people – have a far higher incidence of perfect pitch.

The difference may arise from the greater discrimination between tone of voice exercised when learning to speak Chinese. Others say that effect is genetic and works the other way round – that east Asian people are born with sharper pitch perception and because the Chinese are part of this group they were able to develop a tonal – pitch-sensitive – language. Either way, if you have been speaking Mandarin, Korean or Japanese from an early age, your chances of having perfect pitch will be boosted to one in a thousand. Once again, the connection is there between the voice and the ability to play an instrument. Being good at one tends to mean you are good at the other.

Perfect pitch: are you born with it?

Some academic experts say that unless you are born with perfect pitch, it cannot be learned after the age of about eight or nine. Others say that the process of memorising music can help develop perfect pitch. And still others say it can be learned, even at a relatively late age, by doing exercises designed to train and improve your musical memory. All agree that pitch perception can be improved by playing an instrument, especially a string instrument, where you must listen carefully as you form each note.

Do you have a musical body?

Alongside a desire to learn to play a musical instrument it is worth considering any physical characteristics you have that should be taken into account when choosing an instrument.

If you plan to learn alongside your young children or grandchildren, for example, then their age might be a constraint on the choice you make. An instrument that is difficult to handle, such as the tuba, should be ruled out. Young children will not be able to lift them, and that means you can't learn alongside them. If, however, you plan to learn an instrument on your own – or with other adults – your choices are wider, but there are still potential physical constraints to think about.

What shape are your mouth, lips and skull?

Success in mastering any of the brass or woodwind 'blowing' instruments depends partly on the shape of your lips, teeth, inner mouth and even your skull.

You will be able to produce a warmer and steadier sound if you have a relatively large oral cavity, a high roof to the mouth and strong facial muscles. This may have been the case for Robert Winston in the series. The size of his mouth wasn't measured, but he found that he could produce good clear notes right from his very first lesson. When playing a brass or woodwind instrument, the air is pumped up from your lungs and is stored in your mouth, as a sort of reservoir. Also, the mouth muscles add pressure to the air coming from the lungs, enabling you to increase the instrument's power and allowing you to exert control over the stream of air emerging from your mouth, which creates the notes.

If your lips naturally relax on top of each other with no over- or under-hang and there is a small round hole or groove appearing in the centre, then you have a great advantage when playing a woodwind or brass instrument. If they do not, you might find that two or more openings in the lips emerge when you attempt to make a sound. It will be harder to form the notes and you may tire more easily.

You should also think about the shape and condition of your teeth before deciding to take up a blowing instrument. The ideal is an even set of relatively small teeth which will allow you to make a tight seal on the mouthpiece of your instrument and control the flow of air. Any kind of over- or under-bite (where the top and bottom rows of teeth do not line up) could be a problem. In addition, any gaps in the front of the teeth may prevent you controlling the airflow, and may rule you out from attempting to play the flute in particular.

How deep is your breathing?

To maintain a good sound on a woodwind instrument you need to have good breath and diaphragm control, so it is important to have at least average (adult) lung capacity. So if you have a good pair of lungs and, especially, if you have experience in controlling your breathing – as a result of yoga practice or exercises designed to improve the singing voice – then you may have a significant advantage in taking up a woodwind instrument (see page 48).

At a normal breathing rate, for example, it can be a real strain to play a large baritone saxophone. The most capacious instrument – a French folk woodwind instrument called the bombarde (see page 24) – needed so much air blowing into it, that the player typically had to rest for several minutes to get his breath back after playing a few notes. For the same reason, solos on the tuba or euphonium tend to be rare, very brief and well spaced out.

All woodwind players must learn the special physical skill of breathing from the bottom of the lung cavity using the powerful diaphragm muscle that is used to a far lesser degree in normal everyday breathing. If you have become aware of this muscle already, and have tried to condition and exercise it, you have a head start.

Circular breathing

Taking on one of the more exotic Middle Eastern and Asian wind instruments, such as the Egyptian arghul (a type of wailing flute), entails learning 'circular breathing'. The circular breather learns how to blow out through the lips while breathing in through the nostrils. Try performing this trick right now ... it's not especially easy, is it?

Circular breathing – or 'super controllable breathing' – may have developed out of the deep meditation techniques of Buddhism and Islamic Sufism. The technique was copied by jazz musicians, such as the saxophonist John Coltrane, enabling them to play 'impossibly' long, improvised runs of notes without pausing to take breath.

The world's most famous living circular breathers are the flautist James Galway and jazz and pop saxophonist Kenny G, who is able to hold the same note for up to 45 minutes. This technique is widespread in the Eastern musical tradition. In fact, most reed instruments of North Africa and the Middle East require the player to have mastered the technique of circular breathing.

Experiment with controlled breathing

Stand with your legs a little wider than normal, so that viewed from above your feet extend beyond your shoulders. Bend your knees slightly and relax your muscles.

Bend forwards as though you are about to touch your toes. Push all the air out of your lungs as you bend.

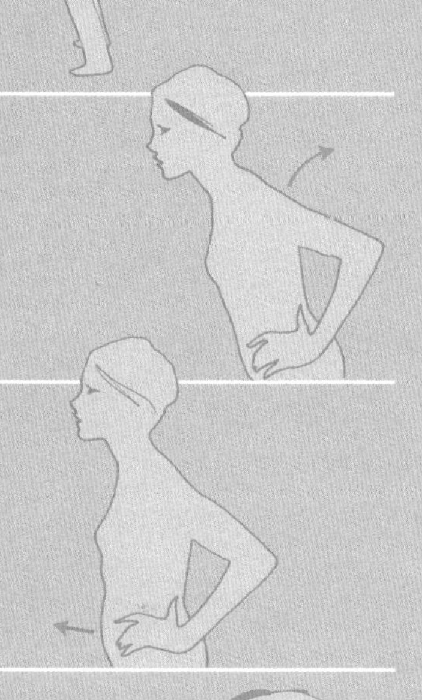

When all the air is gone, begin to breathe in slowly through your nose. Straighten up slowly as you fill your lungs. Bend your knees to protect your back.

Concentrate on the way the air is filling your lungs and, eventually, swelling out your waist.

When you are 'fully inflated' you will feel an urge to breathe out. Instead, hold your breath and count to five. On each count, slowly suck air in again (contrary to your instincts).

After five seconds give in to the urge to breathe out, but let air escape for 10 seconds only. Do not fully deflate as you did at the start of the exercise.

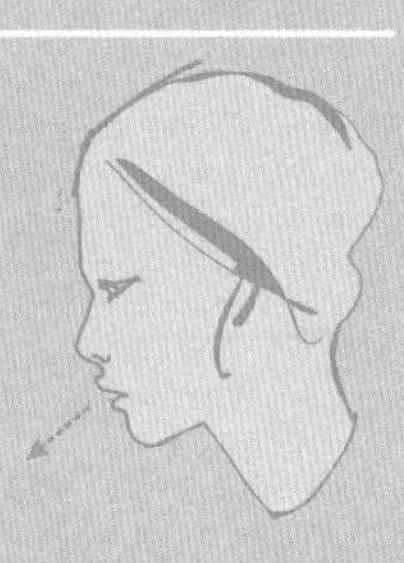

If you feel comfortable with this exercise, you are on your way to mastering the sort of controlled breathing needed in woodwind playing. The idea is to strengthen the diaphragm, a muscle between the stomach and lungs that is not much used in ordinary breathing.

At the same time, exercises like these enable you to keep enough air in your lungs at all times, allowing the body to function without difficulty while, at the same time, breathing in and exhaling additional air to power your instrument. With practice, you may eventually be able to develop super-controlled breathing or 'circular breathing' (see page 46).

While playing a woodwind or brass instrument can be like having a regular cardiovascular workout, you should think carefully if you have asthma. As with specialised breathing exercises, playing a woodwind instrument strengthens the muscles around the lungs and even increases lung capacity, but doctors warn that extensive playing can prompt asthma attacks. If you suffer from other types of lung or throat disease - or if you are a smoker - then you should either seek medical advice or consider taking up a non-blowing instrument.

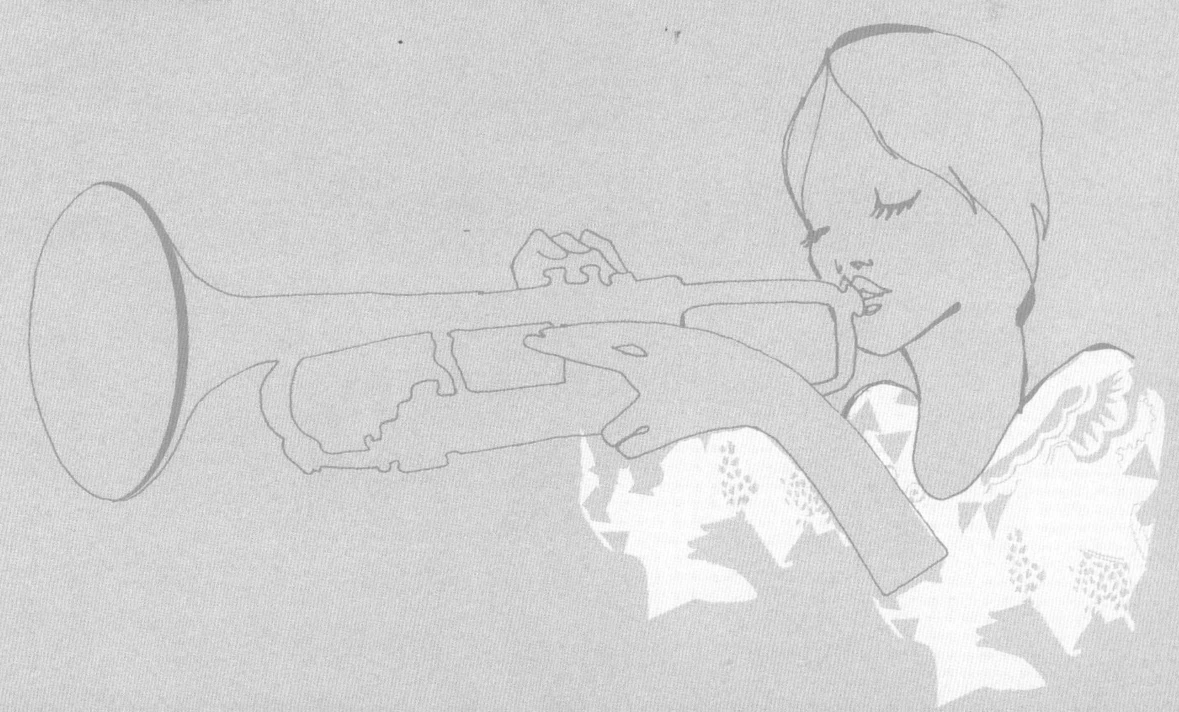

STEINWAY

How flexible are your fingers?

A fair level of finger dexterity is needed to play most musical instruments and for some instruments it is very important. Almost everyone, however, who does not suffer from a specific injury, deformity or disease of the fingers, hands and arms, has enough dexterity to play an instrument. If you have naturally high levels of dexterity and hand-eye co-ordination, or if you have large hands, or long agile fingers, you may have an advantage in playing an instrument such as the piano, guitar, clarinet, saxophone or flute.

Check out your dexterity

You can get a sense of your dexterity by thinking about how well you perform everyday tasks.

Are you good at threading a needle or picking up small objects when they have fallen into difficult crevices?

If you answer 'Yes', then you may well have very fine finger control that is good for piano, violin, guitar and woodwind instruments.

Are you good at catching a ball, throwing darts at a dartboard, playing tennis or table tennis and, generally, have a good sense of balance?

If you answer 'Yes', then you are likely to have good hand-eye co-ordination, which is also good for piano and, in addition, percussion and strings.

Can you touch type?

If you answer 'Yes', then you may have an advantage or a head start in taking on an instrument that requires good levels of dexterity, especially if you found the process of acquiring this skill relatively easy.

Left-handedness can be an issue when learning an instrument, as is the degree of 'handedness' – how strongly one hand is preferred over the other. It probably helps in all music playing to be slightly ambidextrous, since both hands are needed in playing any instrument.

People who have a very big gap between the dexterity of one hand and the other should think about taking up the guitar, violin or another instrument where less dexterity is required in one hand (the one used for plucking or bowing) than the other (required to hold down chords or nimbly finger patterns of notes).

The guitar is the one instrument where left- and right-handed versions are produced and played. Left-handed guitars are widely available these days, the main disadvantage being that they tend to be a little more expensive than their right-handed equivalents. A strongly left-handed guitarist playing on a left-handed guitar, then, would just reverse the roles of the hands. Or she could just continue playing a right-handed guitar, which might be easier in the long run. One of the world's most famous rock guitarists – Jimi Hendrix – played left-handed, using a right-handed guitar held upside down.

If your hands and fingers have been damaged or hardened by your work, then you are more likely to have success with an instrument that requires less fine finger control. While fine finger control is useful in all musical performance, it may be less critical for brass and most percussion instruments. This may be one reason why, in the past, groups of industrial workers like coal miners chose brass and percussion instruments when forming bands. Those instruments require a strong physique, good breathing control and good hand-eye co-ordination, but can still be played with hands that have become even quite badly damaged.

An ability to move your arms independently at different rates and in different directions is also an important skill for playing a jazz or rock drum kit. Unlike the fundamental shape and size of the hands, but as with dexterity, this attribute can be improved with practice.

Some piano teachers test potential students on their ability to move their hands independently. If you can rub the top of your head in one direction with one hand, and rub your stomach in the opposite direction at the same time with the other hand you may have an advantage (most people cannot do this).

'Drumming is more like dancing. You need to get your body doing what your mind wants it to do.'

ALED JONES, PLAY IT AGAIN PARTICIPANT

Long arms and good muscle tone are an advantage for people considering the flute, double bass or trombone (these are useful for violinists and viola players, too), as an element of stretching is involved and the instrument may have to be held perfectly straight for long periods of time.

What's your musical potential?

Ask yourself the following questions and put a tick next to each one that you can answer with a 'Yes'. Then count the number of ticks in each column to determine whether your potential as a musician is erring more towards being a 'natural' than one who has areas that need to be worked on. Of course, learning a musical instrument might be just what you need to do to help you overcome any negative factors that you have ticked.

Positive factors		Negative factors	
Did you enjoy singing as a child?	○	Did you have a bad experience of regimented singing in school?	○
Do you have an expressive and clear speaking voice?	○	Do you tend to mumble and have a monotone speaking style?	○
Do you enjoy listening to and/or speaking poetry?	○	Do you have a functional attitude to language where you are interested mainly in literal content?	○
Do you speak and understand any languages where the tone of voice alters the meaning of words, e.g. Mandarin?	○	Do you enjoy listening to subtle differences in a tone of voice?	○
Do you listen to a variety of types of music?	○	Do you listen to a limited range of music, all with similar tone and form?	○
Do you have normal hearing?	○	Do you have impaired hearing?	○
Do you have good health and nutrition?	○	Do you suffer from asthma or other breathing difficulties and generally have poor health and lack of stamina?	○
Do you have good posture?	○	Do you slouch and/or have back problems?	○
Are you able to or willing to learn to read music?	○	Are you unwilling to learn to read music?	○
Do you tend towards perfect pitch?	○	Do you tend towards tone deafness?	○
Do you have a practice place available?	○	Do you have a practice place available?	○
Do you have the time to practise?	○	Do you have the time to practise?	○
Are you unafraid of failure, and see it as part of the process of learning?	○	Are you afraid of failure and see it as a potential reason to give up whatever you are doing?	○
Total			

'Warm and sexy …
I just think it makes
an astonishing sound.'

 Robert Winston plays the saxophone

Robert Winston plays the saxophone

Robert Winston is one of the most famous and familiar faces on British television as presenter of a series of award-winning documentaries. He is also an active member of the House of Lords and Professor of Fertility Studies at Imperial College School of Medicine in London.

Robert's publishing and media career began in 1986 with the publication of *Infertility – A Sympathetic Approach*. He has since published numerous books and appeared in a host of television series. His groundbreaking BBC documentary series *The Human Body* won several BAFTA awards and his documentary *The Threads of Life*, broadcast in 2001, won the Prix de Jury at the International Science Television Festival in Paris in 2002.

Robert comes from an intellectual family, and music was a big part of that. His father played the violin extremely well and Robert grew up listening to opera on the BBC Third Programme. Later, as a medical student, he was a regular at classical concerts. To further his interest in classical music, Robert later taught himself to read music, so that he could read the score of a classical piece as he was listening to it, increasing his understanding of the piece. But he never found time to learn to play a musical instrument.

LEFT
One step at a time: Robert Winston made immediate progress on the saxophone.

Robert's musical journey

When Robert was assessed for his musical potential at the start of his *Play it Again* challenge it was found that he could just about play 'Twinkle Twinkle Little Star' on the recorder. Undeterred, the target that was set for Robert was the ambitious and nerve-wracking one of playing a saxophone solo during a concert at the Royal Albert Hall.

The saxophone is a modern instrument, most associated with jazz. But it is also used in 20th-century classical music, especially by Russian composers like Shostakovich and Prokofiev. As it happens, these Russian composers are among Robert's favourites. His eyes twinkled as he described the 'disreputable' and even sexy, 'louche' sound of the instrument. He feels that the instrument is particularly good at capturing the soulful, wailing sound of eastern music, including traditional Jewish music. 'The saxophone is close to the human voice,' Robert says. 'It has such a very wide range of expression – I just think it makes an astonishing sound.' It turned out that Robert had a good shape of mouth and teeth for playing a woodwind instrument, so that would not be a barrier to success. He could also get his 'embouchure' – the grip of mouth muscles around the mouthpiece of the instrument – right at once.

During his very first lesson Robert was able to play and sustain strong, clear unwavering notes. Furthermore, his early steps towards mastering the fingering of the saxophone's keys was equally encouraging.

After this impressive start, it was decided that Robert would attempt a fairly advanced piece for performance at the Albert Hall. This was to be Ravel's saxophone arrangement of part of Mussorgsky's *Pictures at an Exhibition*. The piece was one of Robert's favourites, a marvellous, floating and dream-like piece full of bending and wailing notes, with lots of glissandi – sliding phrases where the notes run deliciously into one another. 'He's a very sonically aware person,' said his teacher, John Harle, visiting professor of saxophone at the Guildhall School of Music & Drama in London. 'He could be as lively a musician as he is in all his other areas of endeavour.'

There was even more encouragement after a masterclass session with John Dankworth, the veteran jazz saxophone player. He told Robert to practise blowing long, soft, flute-like notes, sustaining them for as long as he could to improve his breathing technique. 'Breathing is all-important in playing the saxophone,' Dankworth explained. 'It is very close to the rules of yoga, it's all about thinking about how you breathe.

'You have to use your lung muscles continuously and in the right order. It's like the most efficient way of squeezing toothpaste out of the tube. You work it up carefully from the bottom – that's the right way.'

'It's easy to get an edgy sound on the saxophone,' Dankworth concluded, 'but the knack is to get a fuller, more flutey sound out of the instrument.'

Robert was progressing well, but, if anything, he was trying too hard. When struggling, he found that he tended to panic slightly and began to blow harder as he became worried by the prospect of not getting it right. When that happened, his cheeks puffed up, and the increased pressure actually stopped the reed from working. To help him overcome these natural worries, Robert was then introduced to the modern jazz master, Courtney Pine, so that together they could explore the jazz and blues possibilities of the saxophone. He was slightly unnerved by Courtney's insistence that in order to really get the most out of the instrument he needed to turn away, for a while, from reading sheet music and learn to improvise. Pine told Robert that improvisation was all about picking up standard tunes, exploring all their tonal possibilities and moving them on, 'like passing on the baton'.

RIGHT
Robert could already read music, but he had to learn how to improvise.

 Robert Winston plays the saxophone

Pine then showed Robert how to alter his embouchure in order to find and sound notes that are just slightly flat or sharp relative to the normal scale – notes within notes. This technique would open up a whole new side of the instrument – giving him that 'louche' sound he needed to play the movement from Mussorgsky's *Pictures at an Exhibition*.

Going public

After some more practice, it was time for Robert to give his first public performance – an authorised busking session at the foot of an escalator at a London tube station. Together with his teacher playing a portable electronic keyboard, Robert gave vent to 'Greensleeves' followed by a simple classical duet.

He then moved on to play with the National Saxophone Choir (a large number of saxophone specialists playing together) at their annual convention and performance session in a classical concert hall in Birmingham. The aim was to rehearse with the choir, and then perform two pieces with them. In one, Robert would play a simple rhythmic pattern in the chorus, but in the second, he would perform an accompanied duet with an advanced player. Robert was very nervous about performing in public in front of an expert audience of saxophone lovers for the first time. Most of all he was worried that mistakes on his part might make things difficult for other members of the choir, spoiling it for them.

LEFT
Calm and soulful: learning to breath helped Robert to relax.

This exercise was all about learning to play with other people, work in a team and see how the musical contributions of the individual players mingled together to create something new – a sound that was magically more than simply the sum of its parts. In fact, Robert pulled off both tasks very well. He was – as intended – invisible in the chorus role, meaning that he was in tune and did not stand out. The duet was naturally more of a challenge. His tone was a little rasping, but he played his part in time and without a single bum note – a remarkable achievement given his problem with nerves and stage fright. 'I got through it without any major disasters,' he said after the show.

John Harle thought the Birmingham performance was a breakthrough, and a reward for the long hours of practice

Robert had been putting in, often finding time late in the night after the duties of his busy days as a politician, media performer and doctor were over. Robert was also now starting to enjoy himself thoroughly, which would make the whole process of practising and learning much easier and more effective. Birmingham had also introduced Robert to the pleasure of playing in a group.

'I don't want to do this to play an instrument on my own,' he told John Harle. The whole point was to be able to play in a group with others, and he was starting to reach the point where that was becoming a practical reality. He was reaping the rewards of all his hard and systematic practice, but the deadline for the ultra-ambitious target of playing the Ravel solo at the Albert Hall was now closing in.

'With the immensity of the performance, we've really got his attention now,' Harle said. The message that ability had to be built step-by-step was now sinking in. 'He's really got the point that you can't just try and polish it at the end,' the teacher added. 'When he needs to find the ability during the performance, it will be there because all the technical ability has been laid down carefully months before.'

RIGHT
Busking on the London Underground after just a few weeks.

But there would have to be a final push if Robert was going to avoid making a fool of himself in front of a huge live audience at the Albert Hall. This was a man who set himself incredibly high standards, and who was driven to succeed at everything he did. Sometimes it was quite literally a matter of life and death. As his teacher put it: 'He's now driven by fear of failure.'

The final challenge

Robert approached the actual performance with trepidation. He had practised and prepared himself, but there was a problem. To perform the piece, he would have to play at the absolute limit of his ability. He dealt with the psychological pressure by persuading himself that he would probably get one or two notes wrong, but that this didn't matter. What he was attempting to do would be explained to the audience in advance. He knew that he had put in enough work to make a worthwhile effort. It would not be a completely polished performance, but that did not matter. It was the start of his new life as a saxophone player, not the end point.

In fact, Robert's performance was a triumph. He stayed in tune throughout and, although he missed out one or two notes, he kept on playing, so nobody would really have noticed. The tone was good. It wavered and sounded a little raw in places, but it never collapsed and at the end he was cheered to the rafters.

After the performance, Robert was typically self-effacing. 'That was a bit ragged. It was OK – but there's a huge amount of work to be done to be anything like one-fifth as good as the professional musicians you have here at the Royal Albert Hall.' Robert's teacher, on the other hand, had a different verdict: 'That was absolutely terrific. I am thrilled for him. He was under a lot of pressure and he did it.'

From 'Twinkle Twinkle Little Star' on the recorder, to the solo performance of a tricky classical piece on a difficult instrument in front of an expert audience at the home of the last night of the Proms – that's an immense achievement.But Robert Winston was typically modest: 'It is all about the instrument,' he smiled and shook his head: 'I just think it makes an astonishing sound.'

Chapter 3

Which instrument?

An introduction to the different instruments

Before going any further, here is a brief guide to the different groups – or families – of instruments. This chapter then looks at some questions it is best to ask yourself on your quest to discover which instrument might suit you best (see pages 70–89). An overview of each family is then provided to help you narrow your choice still further.

- **Guitars** (see pages 90–3)
- **Piano and other keyboard instruments** (see pages 94–7)
- **String instruments** (see pages 98–101)
- **Woodwind instruments** (see pages 102–9)
- **Brass instruments** (see pages 110–13)
- **Drums** (see pages 114–17)
- **Tuned percussion** (see pages 118–21)

Instruments are classified into groups depending on the ways in which they are made and their basic playing style. The categories originated with the symphony orchestra, which is made up of sections – string (violin, viola, cello and double bass), woodwind (flute, oboe, clarinet, bassoon and associated instruments, but also members of the saxophone family), brass (trumpet, French horn, trombone and tuba) and percussion.

Some instruments, such as the guitar or piano, do not fit easily into these categories, but it is still worth thinking about instruments in groups. Some musical instruments, like the contrabassoon, viola or 12-string guitar are, in effect, just specialized versions of other instruments in the same 'family'. Very often if you wanted to play instruments such as these, you would start with the 'basic' instrument in the same family group – in this case, the bassoon, violin and acoustic or Spanish guitar.

If you decide to explore a particular instrument – or group of instruments – get to know the sound of each one and the range of music available. You may be able to persuade your local musical instrument dealer to demonstrate the instruments to you, if you book an appointment in advance. ▌

The guitar and other plucked string instruments

Acoustic (folk) guitar the basic instrument of this group
Classical ('Spanish') guitar an older version, used in classical music
F-hole jazz guitar a cello-like instrument played with a large plectrum
Semi-acoustic electric guitar and amplifier amplified jazz guitar
Solid body electric guitar and amplifier the class rock instrument
Bass guitar and amplifier a modern alternative to the jazz double bass
Banjo plucked folk and musical hall instrument
Harp plucked orchestral instrument, with folk versions

Piano and other keyboard instruments

Piano the basic instrument of this group
Electronic keyboard amplified piano with built-in microphones and many different synthesised sounds
Organ pipe, reed, electric and electronic versions
Harpsichord early form of piano but strings are plucked and there is no sustaining pedal; specialist

String instruments

Violin the smallest and highest-pitched instrument of this family
Viola very similar to the violin, but with a deeper tonal range; larger hands needed
Cello much lower tonal range
Double bass the largest and deepest-pitched instrument in this family

Woodwind instruments

Flute a soft, melodic tone created by blowing across the head piece
Piccolo a high-pitched flute; specialist
Clarinet a single-reeded instrument that has similar fingering to a recorder
Bass clarinet larger version of the clarinet that plays very deep notes; specialist
Saxophone several types, designed to cover different tonal ranges from low to high
Oboe a double reed instrument with a 'buzzy' sound
Cor anglais very similar to the oboe, but can play lower notes; specialist
Bassoon a large wooden instrument that plays in the same register as the cello
Contrabassoon low-pitched bassoon, played in the double-bass range; specialist
Recorder a simplied form of flute, extensively used in primary schools
Panpipes a simple folk instrument

Brass instruments

Trumpet the basic instrument of this family
Bugle, or basic horn limited instrument, with no valves or fingering
Cornet very similar to trumpet, warmer tone and easier to hold as smaller
French horn lower tonal range than the trumpet
Euphonium tenor-voiced instrument related to the horn
Trombone tone controlled by sliding arm, not valves
Tuba the largest and lowest pitched of the brass instruments

Drums

Drum kit snare drum, bass drum, tom-tom drum, hi-hat and cymbals
Conga/bongo single or double drums played with the hands
Tabala and other world music instruments wide variety of single and multiple hand drums with distinctive tones, sometimes played with specialised bow-like drumsticks

Tuned percussion instruments

Glockenspiel metal bars laid out to resemble a keyboard, hit with a pair of hard mallets
Xylophone wooden bars laid out like a glockenspiel, but lower in pitch; struck with a plastic, wood or rubber mallet
Marimba a larger, deeper version of the xylophone; used in African and world music
Vibraphone similar to a xylophone but with metal keys; can be played electronically to give its distinctive vibrato effect
Timpani kettle drums, used in symphony orchestras and larger percussion ensembles
Steel drums tuned pans originating from Trinidad

Which musical genre do you want to play?

Most of the major instruments of a symphony orchestra (whether from the string, woodwind, brass or percussion sections) can also be used to play jazz, soul, rock, classical, folk and world music. By choosing one of these instruments (the trumpet, for example), you are keeping your musical options open.

Folk music

When it comes to folk music, the **flute** is a mainstay. The **violin** is more prominent in Scottish and Irish music, where it is played as the 'fiddle'. The instrument also has a prominent place in folk-based musical genres like country and western and folk-rock. With other 'folk' instruments, however, like the **banjo**, **accordion**, or **acoustic** or **electric guitar**, you will not be able to easily learn much classical or jazz music, still less have the opportunity to perform it.

Jazz and/or soul

Guitar (in all its many guises), **clarinet**, **sax**, **trumpet**, **double bass** and **drums** are all instruments worth thinking about. Violin and flute less so, though, as these mainstays of the classical world are used less frequently in jazz; their place is taken by both the alto saxophone, solo trumpet and up-front, often female, solo singers with whom the violin (or flute) would clash.

Rock and pop

Well, this is kind of obvious: **guitar**, **keyboards** and **drums** are the mainstay, but there are more unusual combinations such as including an **electric violin** and **cello** in the line-up.

Classical music

If it's classical music that you enjoy listening to and think that you would like to play, any of the instruments outlined on pages 68–9 would be a good bet. The **piano** is the only truly ubiquitous instrument. The standard classically based method of learning the piano will keep all your doors open, preparing you to perform in basically every known musical genre. **I**

> 'Music is genuine and healthy and the stimulation I get from moulding it and adding dynamics is like nothing else on earth.'

BRIAN WILSON, KEY WRITER FOR THE BEACH BOYS

Do you want to accompany yourself or others?

If you have answered 'yes' to accompanying yourself while singing and want to do so comparatively quickly, then you have joined the largest group of music makers in the UK – those who learn to play the guitar. The number of singer-guitarists is vast and growing all the time. The other natural instrument for accompanying yourself is the piano.

The **acoustic** or **folk guitar** has the advantage of being a relatively quick, easy and cheap instrument to learn. With a half decent instrument and a bit of effort you could be accompanying yourself in singing simple folk or pop songs after a couple of days. Some rock guitarists perform in public a few weeks after picking up their instruments for the first time.

The **piano** is harder and more expensive to learn and is impossible to transport (unless you have an electronic keyboard). Unlike the guitar you can't socialise with it or take it with you to, for example, a party or jam session. But it is much more flexible in the sense that you can move much more easily between musical genres and on to more challenging performance pieces as well.

The great thing about a musical accompaniment is that it is bound to make your voice sound much better, no matter how good or bad it is to begin with. This accounts for the popularity of karaoke. People may still sound terrible, but the chances are they would have sounded even worse if they were signing solo without accompaniment.

So by singing along with an instrument, your voice is automatically boosted, with or without training. At the very least, the tone is set for you, so even if you stray off-key as a singer there's an instant reminder that you have done so, as well as an automatic guide back onto the path of tunefulness. The instrument will also fill in any missed notes, and add power, volume and consistency to the overall musical sound. Your voice will automatically sound better.

There are doubtless additional psychological advantages to accompanying your singing with an instrument. Bursting into song in front of others requires confidence. But learn to play the **piano** and suddenly there's three-quarters of a ton of solid mahogany between you and the audience. You can simply hide behind it. Other shy singers may prefer to hide behind a **guitar**, **banjo**, **piano**

accordion or even, like the troubled genius Seventies' American singer Karen Carpenter, a **drum kit**.

Accompanying others

If your aim is to accompany other singers, your choice of instrument is less restricted, but it would be best to take up an instrument normally found in a pop, jazz or folk group. Just beware the popularity of the **guitar**. Fully one-quarter of all amateur musicians in the UK play the guitar, so there is a national glut of players looking for groups to join. There may be as many as 10 guitarists available for every drummer and so it may be difficult to find a group that can accommodate you.

Of course, learning to play an **acoustic guitar** can lead on to the **electric guitar** and the **electric bass**. Even though different playing techniques are used, there is perhaps a greater chance of getting involved in a group (and so accompanying other singers or players) playing either of the latter two instruments. Alternatively, you might be better off mastering a more specialised group instrument, such as the **drums**.

> 'That's what's great about music, you know? With music, when you're down, it's easier to get up.'
>
> ERIC CLAPTON, GUITARIST

Playing for yourself

There are always musicians who enjoy playing entirely for their own pleasure and without feeling the need to play in a group. If this is the case with you, the **piano** has the advantage of being a completely self-contained musical instrument with a vast solo repertoire in all musical genres from nursery rhymes and church hymns through to pop, show tunes, rock, blues, country, soul, reggae and experimental art music. In addition, almost any other instrument would benefit from being accompanied by the piano at some time or other. ■

How practical is it to play an instrument?

Alongside your ambitions, intellectual and physical considerations, you need to think carefully about your personal housing circumstances and even the state of your relationships when choosing an instrument.

Guitar

One key to the success of the guitar is that it is easy to transport, relatively robust and indestructible. **Electric guitars** present even fewer problems in terms of portability and care – because they have solid bodies, they are very hard to damage and are less likely to warp than instruments with sound boxes.

Piano

Unless you live in a mansion, you will have to organise a lot of your living space around the piano. It will also need to be kept at a fairly constant temperature and looked after well. Despite their great weight and apparent solidity, pianos are, in fact, delicate instruments with many moving parts that can go wrong.

String instruments

You can take a **violin** and **viola** to lessons easily and bring it along to group and ensemble sessions. The **cello** and **double bass** are more difficult to move around without risking damage, but you can still do so.

Damp environments

A dank and windowless basement with a few old mattresses piled up against the wall can be the perfect place to practise the drums, electric guitar or other amplified instrument – combining sound-proofing with appropriate rock-chic grunge décor – but do not keep a piano in such a place (or indeed any other acoustic instrument, such as a guitar or string instrument). Damp, very hot or very cold conditions will ruin any instrument that is particularly vulnerable to warping, destroying their tone (or even their ability to be accurately tuned).

Woodwind and brass instruments

Each of these instruments divides into a series of smaller tubes, which take apart. This means you can dismantle the instrument and carry it in a relatively small carrying case. There are few problems in taking your own instrument with you to lessons or travelling to join in with group and ensemble sessions.

Practising issues

Many larger, older houses were designed to have a **piano** in the front room. But in those days the instrument was the only source of entertainment. Today, the piano has to compete for practice space and time with TV and a host of other distractions. Friends and relatives might be supportive of a decision to buy a piano – the instrument can function as an attractive piece of furniture – but they might not be as tolerant of regular practice sessions taking place where they go to relax.

As a single person, you would have a guaranteed practice space for your piano, even if you lived by yourself in a student bed-sit. There would be no family members or partners to complain, but it is very likely that the neighbours would do so in their place. You may think of yourself as having taken up the positive, peaceful and life-enhancing hobby of learning a musical instrument, but without knowing it, you could have become somebody else's neighbour from hell.

Other loud instruments, such as a **string** or **brass** instrument, **drums** or **electric guitar**, will present you with a similar range of problems. There are always mutes for string and brass instruments, and for drums you can buy a set of virtually silent 'practice pads' to place on the top of each drum. **Electronic drums**, which are played with sticks in the same way as a normal drum kit, might also be an answer – you can listen to your playing through headphones.

Dedicated rehearsal venues

If practising at home is completely out of the question, soundproofed professional rehearsal rooms – ample for solo practice, and big enough for a small rock group or chamber music ensemble – can be hired for between £5 and £20 an hour (the most expensive rates are in London) with a piano available.

Alternatively, a local music college or the music department of an adult education college or university, if you have one nearby, may be prepared to let you use a practice room for a small fee. Small rooms in church halls and community centres may be available for hire too, but if they are not soundproofed, there may be constraints on the time and duration of practice session in order to avoid clashes with other users.

Spider

How do you feel about gender stereotyping?

Research shows there is a lot of gender stereotyping associated with particular instruments and, even more, with particular genres played on those instruments. Your own thinking has quite likely been affected by stereotyping.

Research into the musical preferences of school children in the USA (see page 83) has shown that, even these days, few girls would take up relatively common instruments like trumpet, trombone, saxophone or drums without special encouragement. At the same time, both boys and girls thought of the violin, flute, clarinet or cello as being essentially feminine. Their reasons were not so much about the sound of these instruments, but the performance style. Large or brassy instruments, which appear to entail a lot of obvious and apparently strenuous effort to play or carry about, were seen as being 'for boys'.

There may be additional physical constraints for both men and women. Men may, on average, have the larger skull and greater general strength needed for the bigger brass instruments, such as the tuba and larger, deeper sounding varieties of saxophone. Women on average have greater fine motor skills making the piano, woodwind and plucked instruments, like the guitar, banjo or harp, slightly easier to play.

> 'I was the first rock 'n' roll successful female who led a band of men and seriously played an instrument.'
>
> SUZI QUATRO, BASS GUITARIST

Ultimately, however, psychological factors seem to be in control. Eight-year-old girls observed closely at a concert were seen to pay huge amounts of attention to a woman trombone player. They looked at her 37 per cent of the time, as opposed to one per cent of the time spent looking at a male trombone player, which was taken as a sign that they thought her to be odd, unusual or even funny. Both boys and girls with little experience of instruments rank them as being less important and less desirable to play once they have seen a member of the opposite sex using them.

Making a choice

Related research has shown that young people are much more motivated to learn a musical instrument when they believe it to be appropriate to their gender, or to be popular with their peer group. Purely musical factors come second to these considerations. Even subjective feelings about the weight, size, appearance and portability of the instrument, as well as the posture needed to play it, are weighed as factors in making a choice.

It might not help that one of the most famous pieces of classical music played to very young children as an introduction to the world of music and instrumentation is *Peter and the Wolf*. In this piece, the characters and animals are imitated by particular instruments based on their correspondence to adult male or female vocal range.

Male characters, such as the Grandfather, the hunters and the wolf, are represented by the low, powerful notes of bassoon, kettledrums and the French horn. Female characters – a bird, a duck and a sly cat – are represented by 'female' instruments – the flute, oboe and clarinet.

Ideas about gender roles in music making clearly run deep and it might be worth thinking about this as part of your choice of instrument. Bring those feelings that you should not play this or that instrument because it is for the opposite gender to the surface and address them because it might make all the difference as to what you choose to play.

> 'Male or female – if you want to play drums, go for it!'
>
> CAROLINE CORR, DRUMMER, THE CORRS

Exploring gender stereotyping

Jo Brand is playing around with music and gender roles in her quest – and the cheesy double entendre can't be avoided – to play with a massive organ. Diane Abbot has chosen the gender-neutral piano. Aled Jones is making a macho statement in taking up the drums – the opposite end of the gender stereotype from being a boy singing entirely in the female register as a soprano.

Bill Oddie, in gender stereotyping terms, has gone for an uncontroversial choice for a man of his age – in the Fifties and Sixties, the electric guitar was Macho Central, but the instrument's image has mellowed with age. Still, his desire to plug his axe into a 1,000 watts of amplified sound could be seen a sign of mid-life crisis – the musical equivalent of suddenly buying a Harley Davidson motorbike. Frank Skinner's banjo is bloke-ishness in musical form – fitting perfectly with his image as a performer.

Flutes are from Venus, trumpets are from Mars

A 2004 Rutgers University survey of male and female choice of a limited range of instruments in US schools showed very different attitudes on the part of the sexes. It even showed that many boys who said that the flute was their favourite sounding instrument, chose to play a 'boy's' instrument like the trumpet (which relatively few of them actually liked). Many girls, on the other hand, took up the clarinet even though it was not their first choice. The survey excluded the piano, guitar and stringed instruments.

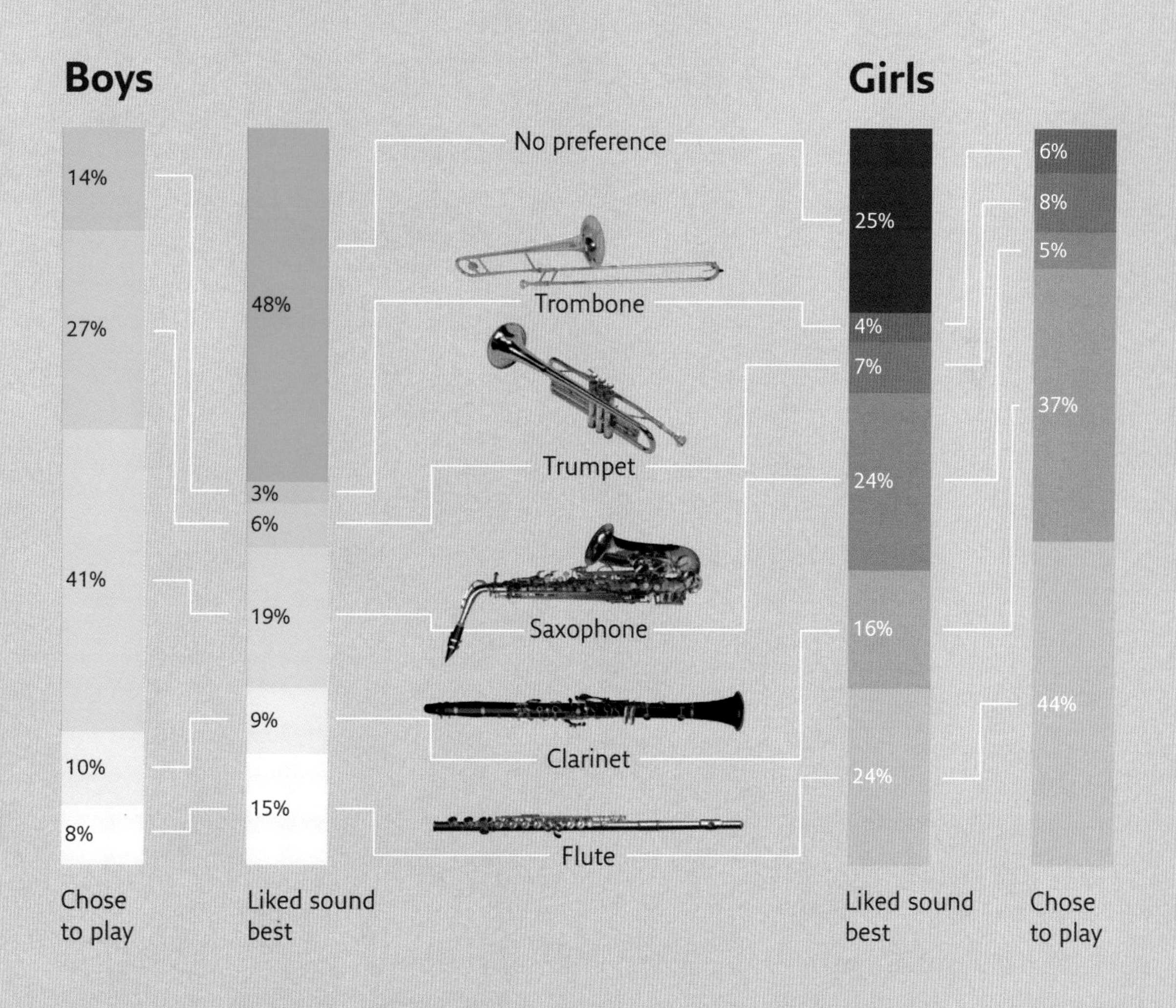

Gibson

Is cost an issue?

Buying a piano can cost thousands of pounds, but other instruments, such as the guitar, are much cheaper. The average cost of a good guitar is under £200, and a new beginner's instrument will cost less than £100. Second-hand instruments can be had for less than that, though you have to be sure you know what you are getting. Then there is the cost of instrument lessons (see page 133).

According to the Office of National Statistics, as a nation we spend an incredible £450 million a year buying musical instrument, parts and accessories. Nearly a quarter of this total is spent on guitars. Nearly one million guitars were bought in 2005 (the last year for which statistics are available) – double the number sold in 1999 – and the music industry is talking about a guitar 'boom' resulting from the over-40s' generation taking up the instrument for the first time. For information on choosing an instrument to buy, see pages 174–95.

Guitar

Cost is not really a barrier to learning the guitar, whereas other plucked string instruments, such as the **harp** and related harp-like folk instruments (like the **zither** or **autoharp**) may be far more expensive. **Banjos** are expensive because they are highly specialised instruments and cannot be mass-produced. The more humble **acoustic guitar** is, however, so popular that hundreds of different varieties and makes are available, ranging from very cheap, mass-produced versions available for under £100 to handmade and custom-designed instruments costing tens of thousands.

Electric guitars can be obtained very cheaply too, though there is the additional cost of amplification to be considered. Good quality amplification is as critical to the sound of an electric guitar as the instrument itself. In fact, you could say that the music of an electric guitar is actually 'made' by the amplifier.

Piano

The main problem with the piano is the cost of buying and maintaining one of sufficient quality to be (and stay) playable. Buying a cheap or wrecked second-hand instrument is a false economy as any aptitude you may have can easily be swamped by attempting to make the instrument sound in any way sweet. The difficulty is that there are vast numbers of such old wrecks on the market, and many of them still look quite attractive and even impressive as furniture.

If you want to buy a reasonable quality new upright piano, you need to think of starting prices around £1,700, with the better-known makes, such as Yamaha, starting at about £2,000. A new baby grand piano would cost around £4,500 and a full-scale concert hall grand piano about £10,000.

Buying second hand is risky – there are just so many things that can go wrong.You should always ensure that a second-hand instrument is carefully examined by the piano tuner you plan to engage to look after your piano. Buying an old piano (say a baby grand for under £1,000) might make sense if it is capable of restoration. A full re-build of an old piano would cost between £3,500 and £4,000 and so the total cost of acquiring a reconditioned piano will work out about the same as buying a new one.

The quality problems that afflict acoustic pianos are less critical for **electronic keyboards**. They have few moving parts and both the notes and tones are created by electronics, in a way similar to the solid body electric guitar. For less than £100 you can buy a full-size keyboard with all manner of supportive software (see page 148).

String instruments

New factory-made **violins** and **cellos** (with bow and case) can be bought for under £100 (slightly more for a cello), and there are no continuing costs except for occasional replacement of strings and rosin, the amber substance rubbed against the bow to make it sticky. You might, however, want to start off by hiring your instrument – a violin can cost less than £10 a month – to see how you get on.

Over time, you might decide that an older, quality string instrument is for you. There are specialist dealers all over the country who will be only too happy to advise you, although in the end it comes down to a personal choice as to the tone that you like. Such a violin will cost anything from £500 to tens of thousands of pounds. However, as with good quality antiques, the instrument should continue to increase in value. If you aren't buying a factory-made 'kit', you will have to pay separately for the instrument, bow and case. As with anything, the better the quality, the higher the price.

Hire purchase

Some instrument suppliers operate hire purchase schemes, or after a year will offer to sell you the instrument you have hired at a heavily discounted price.

Woodwind instruments

As with string instruments, you might decide to rent an instrument first to see how you get on with it. If you hire, you will need to add the cost of insurance to the rental fees. Insurance companies will quote for particular instruments but the cost of insurance can exceed the hire cost for more specialist or expensive models.

You can rent a standard **clarinet** for about £15 per month, but new instruments are expensive. A standard clarinet will cost at least £500 and anything with added niceties, such as silver-plated keys, will cost upwards of £1,000. Plastic versions are much less, but the tone and stability of the notes is not great.

Saxophone rental starts at about £20 a month for an alto, and more like £25 a month for a tenor or baritone instrument. Specialist saxophones, such as the soprano (very high pitched) or bass (very low), are not very suitable for beginners. To buy, the cheapest new saxophones start at about £300 for an alto and £400 for the tenor or baritone. Relatively cheap instruments sound fine for beginners, but they have lower standards of manufacture and tend to wear out more quickly.

Flute rental costs about £15 per month and a new instrument starts at around £150 to buy.

Brass instruments

Trumpets can be hired for about £15 a month and a reasonable quality, student level **trumpet** will cost about £200 to buy. If you have more money to spend on a brass instrument, it might be a good idea to buy a top quality mouthpiece, and attach that to the body of a standard instrument – the effect would be a big increase in playability at relatively little expense.

You will also need to add a one-off cost of up to £30 to buy valve oil, a mouthpiece brush and cleaning snake (there is no escaping the unpleasant fact that brass players, like woodwind players, have to deal with the daily problem of corrosive spit removal).

Drum kit

Drum kits get such a battering – quite literally – that there are few opportunities to hire beginner level kit for practice. The best option, then, is to buy a relatively cheap drum kit, perhaps on hire purchase. A standard kit consisting of bass drum, snare drum, hi-hat, single tom-tom, and two cymbals (crash and snare) can be bought for about £350. The additional cost of superior drum kits comes from higher manufacturing standards. ▌

Narrowing your choice

The guitar

The **acoustic guitar** is a simple piece of ancient technology used to create what amounts to an artificial human voice. The metal or nylon wires (the strings) are stretched tightly across the body and neck of the instrument. When they vibrate, they create sound in a similar way to the vibrations of the human vocal cords.

In the human voice, the vibrations are caused by air passing over and through the cords, a bit like the sound of wind through telegraph wires. The guitar's artificial vocal cords – the strings – are made to vibrate by plucking them with the fingers and thumb of one hand.

Sometimes the strings are gently brushed by the naked fingers and at other times they are struck quite hard with a small piece of wood or plastic called a plectrum to create a harsher, more piano-like sound. The differing ways in which the strings can be made to vibrate gives the guitar (or group of guitar-like instruments) a huge range of expressive tones.

In the human voice, changes in pitch happen when the vocal cords are pulled tighter, to make them shorter and higher-pitched, or loosened to make them longer and lower in pitch. In plucked stringed instruments, this is simulated by using a number of strings of different length. The modern orchestral ('double-action') harp has a large number of strings of differing length, each producing a particular tuned note when plucked (the piano works in a very similar way, but with strings set out on a harp-like frame and hit with 'hammers', each one corresponding to a particular string and operated by its own key set out on the keyboard).

> 'I'm always in awe of how wonderful the guitar is; to be able to conjure up all those moods in such an exciting way.'
>
> JOHN WILLIAMS, CLASSICAL AND BAND GUITARIST

Guitars normally have only six strings (banjos usually have either four or five), each of which are tuned to produce a different note when plucked. To provide extra notes, each of these six strings can be pressed down hard with a finger to shorten it and raise its pitch. By moving the finger up the neck of the instrument, the strings are made shorter and, as a result, higher notes are produced when those strings are plucked.

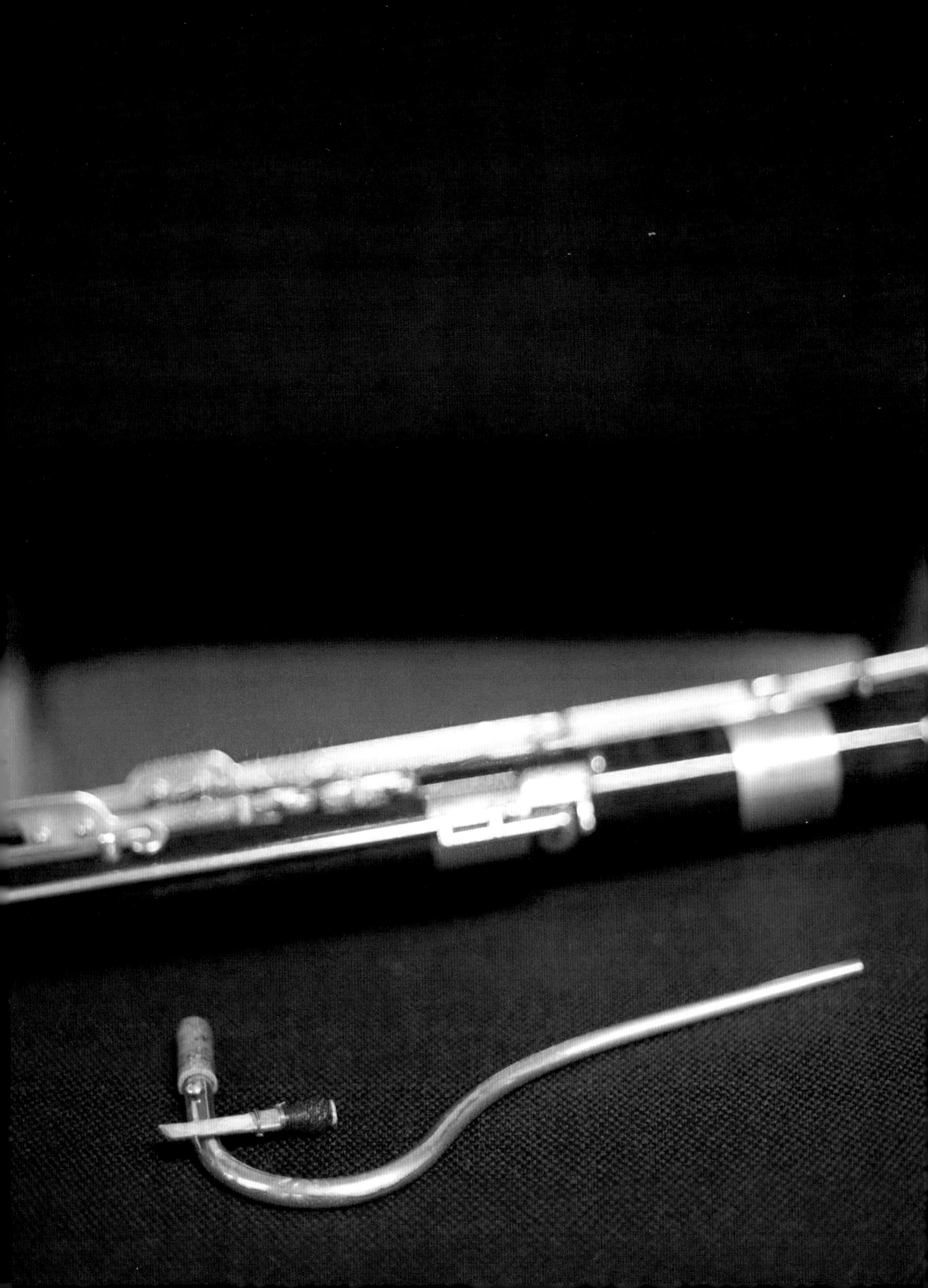

Tokai
Fender TELECASTER

Finally, in the human voice, the tone of the notes produced is amplified and coloured by the shape of the neck, skull, mouth cavity and lips. In the guitar, the same job is done by its box-like body and the round or f-shaped holes cut into it. The size and shape of the guitar's body will affect its tone.

How about an electric guitar?

The electric guitar is a modern instrument, which means that it came far too late for inclusion in the symphony orchestra (or even the classic jazz line-up). This means it is used almost exclusively in pop, rock and blues music. Some types of electric guitar have a shallow acoustic body – known as **semi-acoustic guitars** – which are capable of making a natural sound, which is then amplified and coloured with bass, treble and other effects by the electronics of the amplifier.

Other electric guitars have an entirely solid and non-resonating body. They produce a very 'tinny' and quiet sound when played without amplification. All the sound is created electronically by the amplifier, giving the instrument a great potential range of tone from harsh, cutting, high-pitched sounds similar to a whistle or a piccolo, through a wide range of powerful, human voice-range tones, down to the soft, gentle humming of bass string instruments like the cello.

Electric guitars are also capable of producing notes that last a very long time (sustain) from just a single pluck. Amplifiers can be easily adapted or set electronically to endlessly sustain particular notes – an important musical feat previously only possible with the violin and other bowed instruments.

And, finally, no rock or pop group would be complete without the four-stringed **electric bass guitar**. The instrument evolved from the double bass, which originally provided the bass or 'bottom' in jazz and dance groups. Like the electric guitar, the modern electric bass has a solid, non-resonating body and is silent when it is played unless electronically amplified. ▌

Other plucked stringed instruments

The variation in plucked stringed instruments mainly comes from the varying type of body each instrument has, creating differences in resonance and the sound created. In the **banjo**, the tone is created by a drum-like sheet of parchment stretched over a metal ring attached to the neck. This form of resonance gives the banjo its crisp, dry sound, where each note is picked and dies at once, with no echo, making it a good instrument for accompanying but no for playing melodic lead. Some traditional **folk** or **Spanish guitars** have large, deeply resonating bodies similar to cellos, which create a less crisp but much warmer sound.

Why you might learn to play a guitar

* The cost of buying an instrument is reasonably low in comparison to other instruments (see page 85).
* It's easy to transport.
* Anyone with normal pitch perception will have little difficulty learning to play a guitar as the position of the fingers is indicated by the frets – the small metal strips across the fingerboard.
* It is possible for the beginner to concentrate on developing the dexterity of one hand at a time, starting with fingering chords and patterns of notes on the neck of the instrument and then concentrating on strumming.
* Left-handed instruments are available.
* It's a great choice for anyone who wants to accompany their own singing, or that of others, even if it isn't especially satisfying as a purely solo instrument.
* Great ensemble instrument – perfect for playing in rock, pop, soul, reggae or folk groups.
* A good instrument to take up if you want to compose your own folk or pop songs as they can easily be worked out on a guitar with very limited knowledge of musical theory or ability to read and write music. Such songs can then be arranged for other instruments.
* The bass guitar is quick to learn. If your main ambition is to perform in a group, then the bass is probably the easiest choice short of singing.

Narrowing your choice
The piano

The piano is such a versatile instrument that it can be categorised as either a string instrument (because the sound is created by vibrating strings, as with a harp or violin) or a percussion instrument (because the strings are made to vibrate when they are struck by small hammers controlled by the piano keys). But the instrument is so important to Western music that it is often considered as occupying a whole category of its own.

The piano matured into its modern form during the early part of the 19th century, when it became the dominant instrument first in classical and then in popular music. In musical terms, the 19th and 20th centuries (at least until the invention of electronics) is thought of as 'the age of the piano'.

'The best toy in our house was the piano. Just at hand height, from a very early age that was my world.'

DJANGO BATES, JAZZ PIANIST AND COMPOSER

Whether the instrument is an upright or grand piano, at its core is a heavy, harp-shaped steel frame. Metal wires of steadily increasing length and thickness are stretched on this frame and tuned to match specific musical notes. This is a formidable manufacturing task, since the pressure on the frame is immense.

Quality control

The process of tuning a piano and of keeping it in tune is a challenge, and is very difficult in cheaper or older pianos where the frame may have become cracked or stressed. Unlike violins and good wine, pianos do not tend to improve with age.

In a piano, the notes are created by felt-covered hammers striking wires in response to being pushed up by the keys on the keyboard. The mechanism is delicate and can easily go wrong. If the hammer mechanism has been made cheaply, the movement of the hammers will be harder to control, greatly reducing the sensitivity of the keys in playing quiet notes in particular.

Another factor affecting the sound of a piano is the piano's body. Larger instruments, such as the sort of full-scale grand piano that would fill an entire room in an ordinary suburban house, will have better tone, as will instruments made from seasoned hardwood. The more widespread 'upright' piano (where the

frame is stood on end to save space) will have a more limited tonal range than a grand piano, but may be no more difficult to play if it is of reasonable quality and has been kept in good repair.

Buying a piano that is worth playing will be a significant financial outlay (see pages 85–6) and the instrument will have to be kept in good environmental conditions – not too hot or cold or in any way – otherwise the all-important frame may warp. Once that happens, the instrument is pretty much useless.

How about an electronic keyboard?

There is a huge range of electronic keyboards, which can be a great way to start learning to play an instrument with a keyboard – perhaps start on an electronic keyboard and then move to a piano, if you find you are enjoying yourself.

More expensive electronic keyboards replicate the touch sensitivity of an acoustic keyboard. They also allow you to play the organ, harpsichord, jazz piano – and many other instruments – simply at the push of a button. Some can even harmonise several instruments at once, allowing you to play the sound of a brass band or the string section of a symphony orchestra.

Or the organ?

Traditional **pipe organs** are highly specialist instruments that sound marvellous, but which are far from ideal as instruments for the musical beginner. There are home versions of organs available, but they cost thousands to buy.

In *Play It Again*, comedian Jo Brand took up the organ for a special reason. She is already a pianist and took to the organ because she wanted to play one of her favourite pieces of music, Bach's 'Toccata and Fugue'. She could have mastered the piece on the piano, but had always dreamed of playing it on a huge organ in a darkened cathedral or concert hall. As an experienced pianist, Jo found some difficulty in operating the pedal board, an additional bass note keyboard that is played with the feet. The reward for any pianist, though, is the tremendous tone of the organ. Most are found in churches, but some organs have survived in dance halls, and these amazing instruments even have keys to sound drums, gongs, cymbals, thunderclaps and train whistles.

> 'Being an organist doesn't mean being a humourless spoil-sport; having fun is part of musical life.'
>
> DAME GILLIAN WEIR, ORGANIST

Organs have up to five keyboards – known as manuals – arrayed in steps one above the other. Each key on each of the manuals will play as many as five pipes, and a further system of controls – buttons called 'stops' – are used to bring more pipes into play (producing louder trumpet and brass-like blasting tones) or to restrict the number of pipes, producing a softer, more violin or flute-like sound.

Why you might learn to play the piano

* Although the cost of buying an instrument is comparatively high (see pages 85–6) and it is difficult to transport, you could always start with a cheaper electronic keyboard.
* Unlike the violin, out-of-tune notes aren't an issue. If even a single string drifts out of tune, it will remain out tune until the whole instrument can be re-tuned.
* The piano presents no especial difficulties for people who are left-handed.
* It is an excellent instrument if you want to accompany your own singing or that of others.
* It is also the best instrument on which to compose music.
* The piano keyboard is the standard 'interface' with computers in any sort of music making and composing.
* Huge quantities of music have been composed for the piano and in all musical genres. There is a growing range of piano teaching computer software.
* Most electronic keyboards allow you to 'cheat' while learning, by allowing a built-in computer to play part of a tune (the left-hand chords, for example) so that you can concentrate on learning to play the melody with the right hand.
* If you feel you have relatively poor finger dexterity, then don't let this deter you from taking up a keyboard instrument. There is evidence that dexterity improves in the process of learning to play the piano, and there are also specific hand and finger exercises you can do to improve this part of your technique.

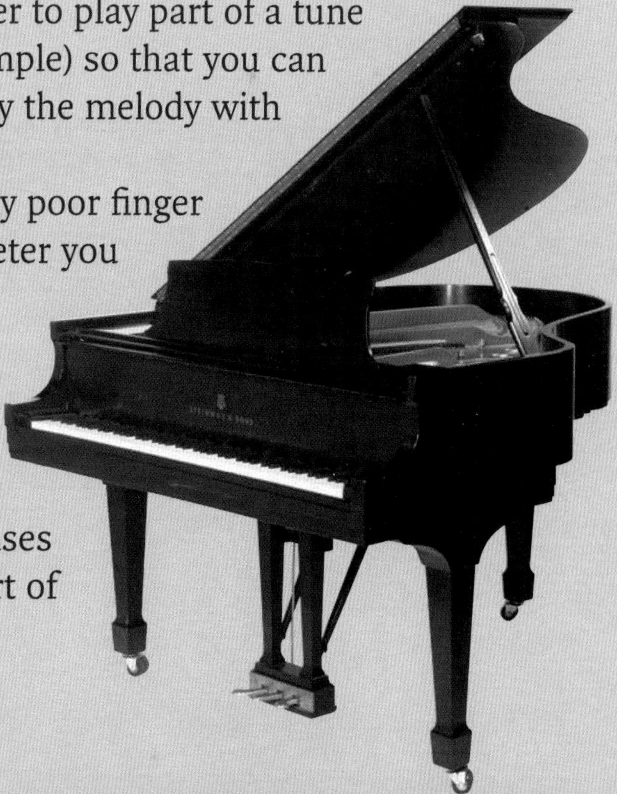

Narrowing your choice

A string instrument

The sound of any string instrument is produced in a way similar to the guitar with the left hand pressing down on strings, altering their effective length and therefore pitch, but with the right hand causing the strings to vibrate through the use of the bow. Each of the instruments in this group – **violin**, **viola**, **cello** and **double bass** – have four strings, as opposed to the six that are normally used on guitars.

A string instrument can be made to sound by plucking the strings with the fingers (as with a guitar) – called 'pizzicato' – but more usually it is played by lightly drawing a bow across the strings. Although it is predominantly one string that is played at a time, chords of up to four notes can also be played. The bow is a thin length of wood with strands of horsehair stretched from one end to the other. Friction causes the strings to vibrate, creating notes. These are then amplified by the characteristic f-holes in the instrument's rigid wooden body.

> 'I have the same feeling when I walk in a very beautiful place that I have when I play and it goes right.'
>
> JACQUELINE DU PRE, CELLIST

String instruments are important in classical music because they can produce a long, continuous note without stopping to take a breath or pluck the string again. In theory, the note produced by a stringed instrument could go on forever. In this way, it surpasses even the voice and so it has long been associated in classical music with the esoteric, the eternal and the mysterious. The fact that notes can so easily be changed in tonal quality and character make them ideal as both the melodic (violins) and rhythmical (cellos and double basses) core of an orchestra.

There is also a huge tradition of solo, small ensemble – especially the string quartet, which comprises two violins, viola and cello – and accompanied violin, viola, cello and double bass playing in classical music. The violin is also a mainstay of folk music and world music. It sometimes features in jazz and, in an electrified form, rock and pop music. Take up any of these instruments and you will always find somewhere to play – once you've reached a certain level, any amateur orchestra will snap you up. This is especially true of viola players, who are a

comparatively rare breed. You will have to develop a thick skin, however, because for some unknown reason viola players are always the butt of orchestral jokes.

How about the double bass?

As well as being an essential part of the orchestra, the double bass was crucial for playing jazz where it was normally (but not always) plucked rather than bowed. From the 1950s onwards, double basses were often replaced in jazz ensembles by electric bass guitars, which are much easier to play and – just as importantly – far easier to maintain. The double bass was also sometimes used as a plucked instrument in the early days of rock and roll (or 'rockabilly'), but has increasingly been replaced by the electric bass guitar. However, if this is instrument for you, there are bands out there looking for the authentic double bass player. **I**

Why you might learn to play a string instrument

* You have good finger dexterity (see page 51).
* The cost of buying an instrument is reasonably low (see page 86) and violins and violas, in particular, are easy to transport.
* It's also possible to hire instruments when starting to play.
* If you are planning to learn at the same time as school-age children in your family (particularly the under eights), then it may be your best choice as you could get involved in a Suzuki-type teaching programme (see page 133).
* If you have a child who wants to learn with you, violins and cellos as small as a one-sixteenth size are available, which means that children can start to play at a very young age.
* There is a wide tradition of solo playing of all the instruments in this family (less so the double bass), though they are often written with a piano accompaniment.
* You have reasonably good pitch discrimination, but if you feel that it could be better, one advantage of learning to play a string instrument is that it will almost certainly train and improve your sense of pitch.
* There are large communities of learners in both the classical and folk genres, so if part of your aim in learning an instrument is widening your social horizons, then a string instrument is an excellent choice.
* Competent players of these instruments are always in demand in amateur groups playing to a good standard.

Narrowing your choice

A woodwind instrument

Woodwind instruments are closest to the natural action of the vocal chords, and sound most like human singing when played well – think of the heartbreaking and plangent strains of Mozart's Clarinet Concerto; or the yelping, laughing, whooping sound of the clarinet in Klesmer music.

A reeded instrument?

Players of woodwind reed instruments produce sound by blowing through a thin piece of wood ('the reed'), which is clamped rigidly in place at one end by a special clip in the mouthpiece of the instrument. You can produce the same effect by cupping a blade of grass or a thin strip of paper in your hands, securing it with the thumbs and palms. If you blow hard across the blade of grass, and if it is held firmly enough, it vibrates, creating a short-lasting rasping note.

The more widely used instruments in this group, the **clarinet** and **saxophones** of various types, use a single reed and this produces a relatively soft and deep initial tone. The others, characterised by the **oboe** and **bassoon**, use a double reed, which produces a slightly more rasping, buzzy tone – still highly vocal and expressive, but with a more quivering and almost tearful emotional edge to it. Probably the most well-known piece of cor anglais (the oboe's larger cousin) music is the solo in Dvořák's 'New World' Symphony, known to millions as the music from the vintage Hovis advert. The vibrations created by air blown through the reed cause a column of air inside the tubular bodies of these instruments to resonate, creating a musical note. In a sense, this column of air is like the vibrating wire of a string instrument – the longer the column, the deeper the note. The vibrating air column is lengthened and shortened by placing the fingers over a series of air holes.

> 'I look upon the oboe as an extension of the vocal cords. I talk through it.'
>
> LEON GOOSSENS, OBOIST

Unlike the **recorder** (see page 108), there are more holes than fingers, and some of them (especially on the **bass saxophones** and **bassoons**) are well beyond the natural reach of a human hand. Instead the holes are opened and closed using a series of levers and covers.

Although originally designed in the 1840s to be played in symphony orchestras, the **saxophone** is a vastly important instrument (or, actually, sub-family, because there are 14 different types of saxophones, all played in a similar way) in jazz and is also widely used in rock music. In classical music, the 20th-century composers Prokofiev and Shostakovich used the instrument extensively and included it in their orchestral line-ups. If you are interested in taking up the saxophone, it might be a good idea to start on the **clarinet**. The instrument works in the same way but, because it is smaller than most types of saxophones, it is easier to handle.

The power of all reed instruments, and especially the saxophone, is the ability to mimic the human voice to a remarkable extent. In jazz, the saxophone is often used to substitute for a singer and, in fact, the tonal effect is very similar to abstract 'scat' jazz singing. In pop music, the saxophone is very often used to echo and strengthen the melodic line of the singer.

The difficulty for players of these instruments is that, as with the voice itself, each note must be produced. The notes are not 'pre-embedded' as they are in a piano, or even the guitar, waiting to be played. Unless you can get the knack of making the initial sound with your mouth and the reed, you will not get past first base. Some people find it difficult to persuade 'clean' notes to emerge from their instrument, especially at first.

The **oboe** and **bassoon** have never really played much of a role in rock, jazz or folk music, so if you are thinking of learning one of these instruments, it is mainly the classical repertoire that you will concentrate on.

More specialist reed instruments

While the clarinet, tenor saxophone, oboe and bassoon are the most popular of the reeded instruments, there are more specialist instruments that you could move on to in due course. If you play the **bass clarinet**, any one of a number of smaller or larger **saxophones**, **cor anglais** or **contrabassoon** you will always be in demand for an ensemble. Be warned, though – they are expensive instruments to buy.

Or a non-reeded woodwind instrument?

In a **flute**, the sound is produced by pursing the lips to blow a stream of air against the edge of a hole – known as the embouchure hole (which is also the name given to the shape of the lips when blowing into the flute) – in the mouthpiece. When the air stream hits this hard edge, it splits in two, like water negotiating its way around a boulder in a fast-moving stream. Air eddies are then set up, which cause the column of air in the attached hollow pipe of the flute to vibrate, creating a musical note. You can get the same effect by directing a stream of air from your lips against the top of an open bottle.

As with reed-based woodwind instruments, such as the clarinet – but unlike an empty wine bottle – the pitch of each note is changed by opening and closing finger holes along the length of the instrument. Also like the clarinet, there are many more holes than fingers on the flute and so there is a complex mechanism of levers to be mastered.

The flute is a vital component of the symphony orchestra, able to carry the main melody, harmonise and add by turns a staccato or smooth layer of tone to the overall sound of an orchestra's woodwind section. It is also sometimes used in jazz, but rarely. And nor has the instrument found a regular place for itself in pop music. The beauty of the flute is its breathy, sustained, gentle and other-worldly tones. That sort of sound does not blend well with the thundering power chords of rock music or pounding rhythms of jazz, funk and dance music.

The beautiful tones of really good flute music can, in themselves, be hypnotic and the instrument and its ethereal sound is strongly associated with the New Age and 'Chill Out' movements. Solo flute music is often marketed as having therapeutic stress-relieving properties over and above those of other instruments. The slim elegance and intricate craftsmanship of the instrument may appeal to many as an accessory to an elegant New Age lifestyle.

The **piccolo**, a smaller instrument that produces notes and is fingered in the same way as the flute, can reach an octave above the top range of its close relation. Operating in this extreme treble range, the piccolo can almost be considered an orchestral 'special effect' rather than a solo instrument, used for the important but highly specialised job of adding a brilliant and penetrating gloss to the top notes in symphonic music. It isn't an instrument to start learning on – orchestral players wear earplugs when playing its highest notes.

'My personal approach is that music should touch the listener at all times.'

JAMES GALWAY, FLAUTIST

In folk music, the tonal range of the flute is normally taken by a traditional instrument, such as the penny whistle or a pipe-type instrument. Almost every folk music culture in the world features a flute-type instrument, very often simply hollow ceramic spheres with blowing and fingering holes punched in the side. The most famous flute-type sound is probably produced by the **panpipes** of the South American Andes. This instrument produces a note in a very similar way to the flute, but instead of controlling pitch with a series of holes in a single pipe, there is a series of pipes, each with a fixed pitch. Each pipe is played in turn, producing the characteristic staccato, breathy sound.

As a child you may have been given a **recorder** to play at school. It is most likely to have been the descant recorder and the sort of music you would have played is unlikely to have been exciting and perhaps a little on the shrill side. However, the descant recorder is but one of a large family, ranging from the 'garklein', which is too small for adult fingers to play with ease, to the contrabass in F, which is about two metres tall.

Playing a recorder does have its limitations in that there isn't a great deal of solo music, but if you enjoy the music of Bach, Purcell and Vivaldi and like the thought of playing in a small, specialist ensemble, then this might be the instrument for you. It is also easy to play alongside younger members of your family, and so you can learn to play this very basic instrument, and even experiment with simple harmonisation, alongside your children and grandchildren. ■

Why you might learn to play a woodwind instrument

* You have good breath control (see pages 46–9) and finger dexterity (see page 50).
* You have suitably shaped mouth, lips and teeth (see pages 45–6).
* You have reasonable pitch perception (see pages 41–2), which is important because of the need to correct any slightly sharp or flat notes. However, learning one of these instruments is a good way to develop a better musical ear because of the need to listen to the quality of sound you are producing.
* The instruments are readily portable.
* You want to play in an ensemble. The clarinet and sax have a long tradition in the world of jazz and all woodwind instruments shine out in classical music.
* Woodwind instruments are not especially delicate and, while they do require careful handling, they are unlikely to crack or warp.
* If you enjoyed playing the recorder at school, then the flute could be a natural progression. The two instruments have similar fingering – at least until you start to play higher notes on the flute.

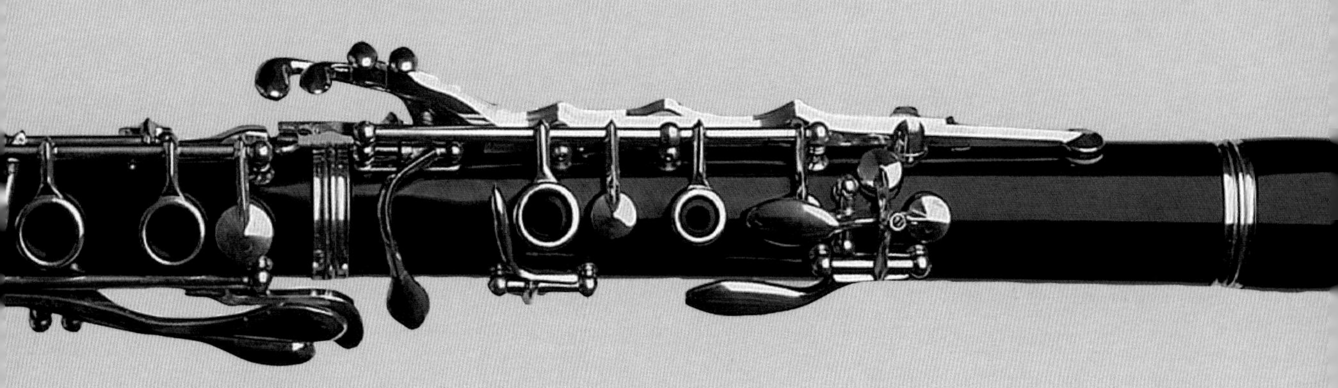

Narrowing your choice

A brass instrument

The brass player produces sound by making the lips vibrate ('blowing a raspberry') against a mouthpiece. This causes vibrating air to pass through a narrow passage in the centre of the mouthpiece, resulting in the air in the body of the instrument vibrating. The player's lips act like the reed in a woodwind instrument (see page 102). For this reason, brass instruments are sometimes described as 'lip-vibrated' instruments.

Different notes are produced by changing the shape of the lips (as in a **bugle**, **antique trumpet**, **hunting horn** or **alpenhorn**) or, more usually, by a combination of changing lip shape and fingering of valves attached to the body of the instrument. In the case of one instrument – the **trombone** – the length of the tube is changed not by manipulating valves, but by sliding a piece of pipe in and out of the body of the instrument, thus altering the length of the vibrating column of air and therefore its pitch.

'Music is more specific than your voice. Everything about you is in every note.'

WYNTON MARSALIS, JAZZ TRUMPETER AND COMPOSER

Brass instruments are not ideal for accompanying your voice or that of somebody else. They are the archetypal ensemble instruments, even though classical solo music has been written for the **trumpet** and **French horn**, in particular. The trumpet is a vital instrument in the line-up of a standard jazz ensemble, and the trombone is often featured in jazz as a lead, solo and 'side' instrument. Brass 'sections' (small ensembles that cover a fuller, voice-like range of tone) are widely used in pop, rock and soul music – although artificial brass sections can easily be created and played on synthesisers and other types of electronic keyboard.

Playing a brass instrument such as the **trumpet** can open up the world of brass band playing. This was originally the preserve of a male-dominated, northern working class and trade union musical culture based around 'works bands' affiliated with particular factories or mines. However, the brass band movement has recently bloomed both at school level (an alternative to the more difficult proposition of running a strings and woodwind-led school orchestra) and on the amateur scene. Brass bands are like orchestral ensembles where the string and

woodwind sections are substituted by their tonal brass equivalents – tuba for double bass, euphonium for cello and bassoon, trumpet for violin and clarinet, and so on.

A disadvantage of playing a brass instrument is that while the trumpet is one of the smaller instruments and relatively easy to transport and maintain, the larger instruments are real monsters – heavy and awkward to transport and to play. Larger instruments from the **French horn** upwards also tend to be on the pricey side because of the tremendous amount of engineering and craftsmanship involved in producing them.

All the brass instruments are great fun to play – noisy, boisterous, joyful, even faintly slapstick and comical (as in the case of the harumpfing tubas and mad-looking sliding arm of the trombone). Brass is as much the music of the circus, the New Orleans funeral, the Salvation Army and the beer hall, as it is of the drawing room or concert hall.

Why you might learn to play a brass instrument

* You have good breath control (see pages 46–9). Players of the larger, lower-toned instrument, such as the tuba and euphonium, in particular, have to be capable of filling their instruments with very large quantities of air to produce full notes.
* You have suitably shaped mouth, lips and teeth (see pages 45–6).
* You have reasonable pitch perception (see pages 41–2), which is important as you need to master the difficult knack of using your lips as a 'reed' to produce the sound and change the shape of your mouth to play the notes in tune.
* Your finger dexterity isn't all that it could be (see pages 51–2) – brass instruments generally only have three valves to manipulate and the patterns in which they have to be pressed in order to produce particular notes are easy for most people to memorise.
* You want to play in an ensemble – brass band and classical music pieces abound.

Narrowing your choice

The drums

Melodic instruments like the violin and clarinet mimic the action of the vocal cords, and brass and flutes mimic the human action of humming or whistling with the lips. Drums work in a very different way – they reproduce and amplify the thumping, pounding sound of the heart. The whole approach to playing the instrument is different.

The basic form of a drum is a cylinder of some sort with a skin stretched tightly over one end. The other end can be left open, or used to amplify and project the sound, or closed off, depending on the type of sound desired. Originally, the all-important skin of the drum would have been taken from an animal. Traditional conga-type drums from Africa and tabala drums from India sometimes still use goat skin. Until fairly recently, the drums used in an orchestra or arranged as a drum kit in jazz or rock playing used fine calf skin. Today, a specially developed plastic is normally used.

> 'Drumming is more like dancing. You need to get your body working.'
>
> ALED JONES, PLAY IT AGAIN PARTICIPANT

When the skin of the drum is struck – either with the naked hand, foot or with a drumstick – the skin vibrates, producing a sudden pulse of sound, which decays smoothly or quickly. The physical action is very like the spasm movement of the heart muscle as it pumps.

Drums fall within the musical category of percussion instruments – the same group as the **piano**, the **xylophone**, **cymbals** and the kettle drum **timpani** of the symphony orchestra. But there is a further sub-division. What we normally think of as drums are 'indefinite pitch' instruments, meaning the sound they make is a mixture of tones, with no particular pitch. The tonal effect of hitting a drum is more like pressing down all the keys of a piano at the same time. Having said that, drummers can tighten or loosen the skins of their drums to shift the pitch up or down, creating either a crisper, 'tighter' sound or a deeper, louder but more muddy effect. A 'tight' drum produces a sound analogous to pressing down all the high keys of a piano at the same time. A loose drum sound uses the lower notes.

Some drums are made so that the pitch range can be altered while they are being played by tightening and loosening the skin as it is being hit. The large

'talking' conga-type drums of African music are 'tuned' to be very loose and are tightened or loosened by the player, pressing down hard with one drum stick as he beats with another. But none of this is not the same as tuning the instrument to a particular note. Because of this, drums cannot be used to imitate the subtle rising and falling tones of human speech, and therefore can't be used to play melody.

The classic drum kit

The classic drum kit consists of a **bass drum**, normally operated with a foot pedal leaving the hands free to play the **snare** and **tom-tom drums** and a range of **cymbals** with a pair of drumsticks. Extra brightness is added to the sound of snare drums by thin chains that vibrate against the skin, creating a very high-pitched, hissing-type sound. The regular alternation of the low tones of the bass drum and the tight, higher-pitched sound of the snare drum is the key to producing the prominent beat that is crucial in pop and rock music.

The attraction of a good clean drum sound is that the instrument creates very little 'sustain' – the sound dies quickly after it is made so that a clear interval of silence is achieved before the next beat comes along. Drummers soften this harsh, un-sustained quality by using cymbals, which resonate long after they have been hit. The pair of **'hi-hat' cymbals** (smaller cymbals that are laid flat, one on top of the other) are a crucial part of any drum kit. They are open and closed by a lever operated by the right foot, marking out the basic beat with a high-pitched clicking, swishing sound synchronised with the beat of the bass and snare drums.

Other types of drum

There are hundreds of different drums produced by every culture on Earth. Non-European drums have become increasingly widely used in pop, rock, jazz and, above all, folk and world music. The **conga** or **tumba drum** is African – or Afro-Cuban – in origin and can sometimes be played with variable tone, like a talking drum. The instrument found a place first of all in Latin American jazz and dance music (where it is often the lead percussion instrument).

The twin-toned **bongo drums** work in a similar way, replicating the alternation between bass and snare in the conventional drum kit. Because these instruments are played by the fingertips and palms of the hands, their tonal range can be changed as they are played.

Less common in the mainstream is the Indian **tabala-bhaya** ('high-low') drum, a wonderful percussion instrument where the tone is altered both by the shape of the hands of the player and by stretching the skin of the drum with a lever as it is being played. Beyond this there is a vast array of non-tuned percussion instruments, such as the **tambourine** and **maracas**, which a person trained on the drums will have no difficulty in mastering. ▌

Why you might learn to play the drums

* You have a strong sense of rhythm and 'timing' and you are able to move your hands independently of each other (see page 52).
* You have good overall physical strength and suppleness.
* You have a strong affinity with pop, soul, rock and jazz, and want to play in an ensemble.
* Drum kits are also used in brass bands, and the snare drum and bass drum are used individually in marching bands.
* You can use your skills to play folk and world music. An interest in classical Indian music is growing all the time and beginning to cross over to mainstream British audiences.

Narrowing your choice

Tuned percussion

The instruments in this group consist of one or more pre-tuned metal or wooden surfaces that create a note of defined pitch when they are hit with a drumstick. The exceptions are the orchestral **timpani** – tuned kettle drums – and the **steel drums**, where different points on the same metal object (originally the top of an oil drum) are tuned to produce distinct and fixed notes.

The **glockenspiel** uses two rows of polished steel bars, each of which is tuned to produce a particular note when hit. The arrangement is similar to the keyboard of a piano, with the 'black' keys being set a little higher than the rest. It is played with two mallets, with one in each hand. The instrument, like most in this group, therefore shares some of the playing characteristics of both the drums and the piano.

> 'The thing about playing percussion is that you can create all these emotions.'
>
> DAME EVELYN GLENNIE, PERCUSSIONIST

The glockenspiel is a high-pitched instrument with a tone that isn't very varied. As the notes are pre-embedded, though, it makes a pleasing, musical sound straight away. Many toy instruments made for children are based on the acoustic principals of the glockenspiel (or 'bells' as the instrument is often call in the USA).

Other instruments laid out like a keyboard are the **xylophone** (which is similar to the glockenspiel but with wooden bars), marimba and vibraphone. The xylophone is another well-established orchestral instrument and is also often heard supporting the meoldy on pop records. The **marimba** uses wooden blocks and drum-like tubes to produce a beautiful, resonating mid-range sound. The **bass marimba**, played with large soft or muffled mallet, is often used instead of a bass guitar or double bass in African and Latin American music. The ethereal **vibraphone** produces vibrato by using an electric motor to stroke the metal sounding bars after they have been struck, resulting in notes that are bright and bell-like before decaying into a warbling sustain. The effect can be quite magical.

All of these instruments are designed to add special colours and tones to the palette of classical, jazz or pop music. But they are hardly essential to any line-up (with the exception of the importance of the bass marimba to Latin and African folk music). They are ensemble instruments, which many ensembles find they can

do without. Likewise, because of the limited tonal range, however attractive that might in its own right, none of these instruments are of much use as solo instruments. At least not for a beginner.

The West Indian innovation of **steel drumming** clearly has roots stretching back to an African tradition. Steel drums were originally made from oil drums and function like deep bass drums when they are empty and one end has been removed. Because the 'skin' of this drum was made of metal instead of animal hide or plastic it was found that it could be tuned to sound a particular note by altering its shape. Further, if the length of the drum was shortened by sawing off the top quarter or so of the oil drum it would produce the same note several octaves higher. Pans come in four sizes: treble, alto, tenor and bass. The higher pitched pans have more notes tuned into them.

Ensembles of steel instruments, each played by a different person, add a new and extremely popular flavour to the world's musical palette – the evocative sound of the steel band is something like the warmer tones of brass powered by the dynamism of the bass marimba. Sometimes the bass pans are supplemented by an electric bass guitar. Very often, as with a brass band, a drum kit is added. **I**

Why you might learn to play tuned percussion

* You have a strong sense of rhythm and 'timing' and you are able to move your hands independently of each other (see page 52).
* You have good overall physical strength and suppleness.
* If you want to play an instrument that is relatively cheap to buy and easy to learn, look to the glockenspiel. It is then easy to progress to another instrument in this family, such as the xylophone or the marimba. It can also make progression onto the piano easier.
* For lively ensemble playing, playing a steel instrument is hard to beat. Many bands exist in British towns, especially in London where Europe's biggest annual street festival – the Notting Hill Carnival – is at core a public competition between rival steel bands from around the country.

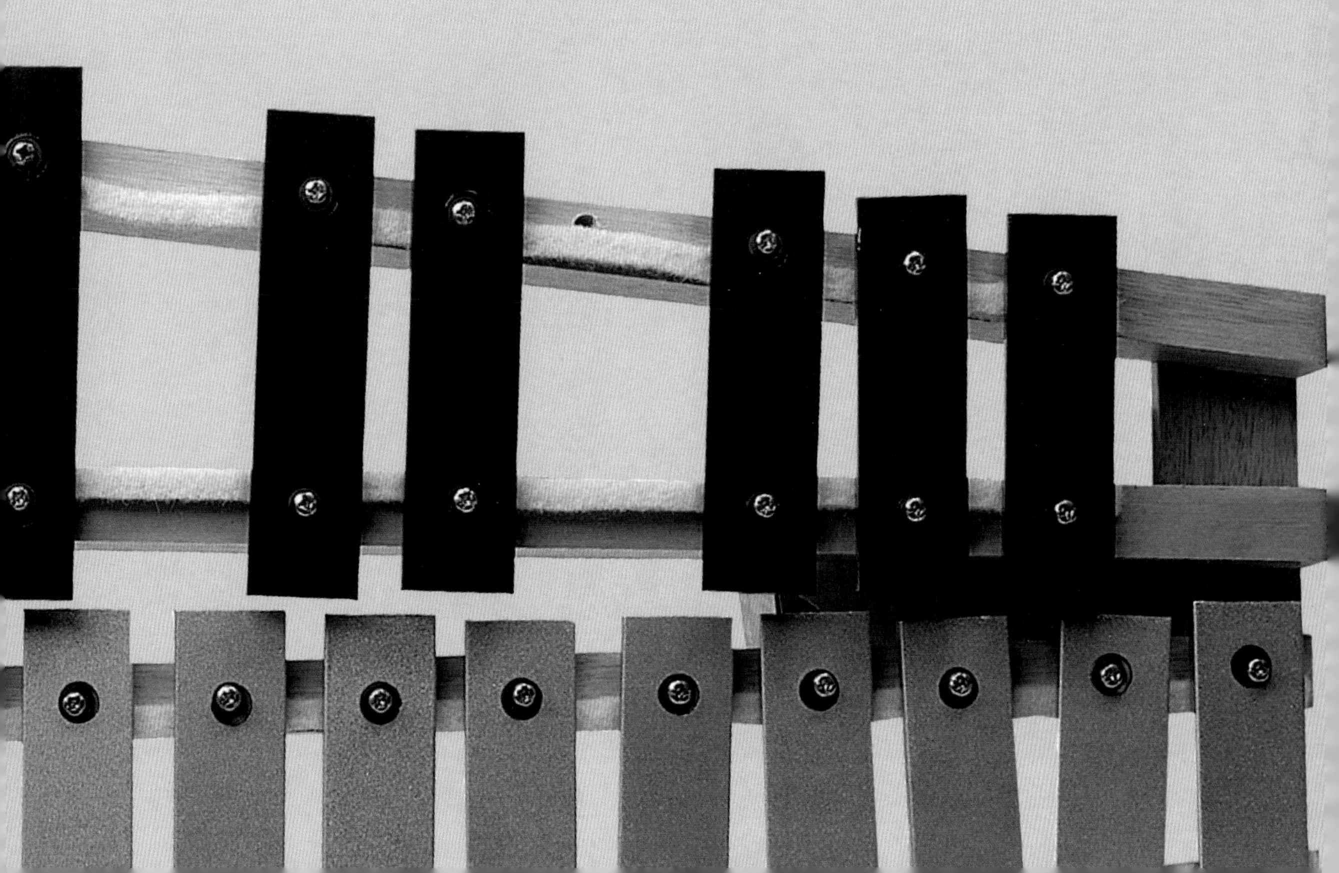

‘I have this nightmare vision of there being silence at the end of it before somebody shouts: “Bollocks!”.’

Jo Brand plays the organ

Jo Brand was a pioneer of the alternative comedy scene in the late 1980s, even though she only started performing live stand-up comedy at the relatively late age of 29. She subsequently became a household name in 1993 after the success of her TV series *Through the Cakehole*. The show was powered by Jo's razor sharp put-downs of male pomposity and the absurdity of traditional gender roles. Numerous TV comedy shows, appearances and series followed, often based on her live stage show. Since then Jo has moved into the mainstream, fronting shows such as BBC1's *Commercial Breakdown* and reaching an ever-wider audience.

Jo falls into the category of people who learn to play the piano as children, but give up partly because they don't enjoy the lessons. In fact, she grew up in a highly musical family. Her father was a talented violinist and the family home was filled with music – Jo remembers the Mendelssohn Violin Concerto, the singing of Paul Robeson and lots of opera. Her mother's favourite was *La Bohème*.

LEFT
Having a ball: Jo Brand gets ready to perform.

Jo started piano lessons when she was still at primary school, and continued until her teens. She reached grade six and could play a wide range of classical pieces by Bach, Mozart and others. She enjoyed some of it, but basically had to be forced to practise. 'It was not an entirely joyful experience,' Jo remembers. 'My first piano teacher was a sweet old lady with white hair in a bun. I used to think that she must be about 150 years old. Then my second teacher was more ferocious – she would hit me on the back of my hand if I didn't put my fingers in the right position. Just a little tap. But you wouldn't get away with that now.'

Jo enjoyed some of her musical training, but found a lot of the practice boring and routine, and by her mid-teens she was starting to rebel. She and her brothers were not allowed to watch *Top of the Pops*, which her mum said was tacky and subversive. As a result, the young Jo felt she was a bit of an outcast at school, a bit of an outsider. She would buy Beatles sheet music and other pop music on the sly, go off on her own, read and play those: 'It wasn't exactly a secret, but it wasn't entirely approved of either. It wasn't "proper music".'

At secondary school, Jo had been forced to take up violin as well as piano, following in her father's footsteps. She came to hate playing the instrument after a teacher forced her to perform in front of the whole school when she was not ready: 'I didn't perform very well. I made a hideous sound – I was so nervous and so angry I gave up the violin. The moral of the story is that teachers need to be sensitive to a child's fears – I was upset and embarrassed – not a great combination at age 11.'

Soon afterwards, Jo's family moved to Hastings and family life became more complicated. There were arguments and eventually she gave up both the violin and the piano – 'the things my mum and dad wanted me to do more than anything else.' Soon after that she went 'off the rails', as Jo now thinks of it, in a blaze of teenage rebellion.

'I have strong memories of jumping out of the window to go to the pub, of being pulled out of the pub by my dad in front of all my friends, and of him punching my boyfriend flat on the pavement for bringing me home late. And me locking myself in my room playing Neil Young's "Only Love Can Break Your Heart" – typical teenage angst music to drown out the parents quarrelling downstairs.'

She left home and that meant turning her back on the formal musical education that had come to symbolise her childhood. 'When I left, that was it for the piano,' she says. 'On one level it is a practical thing. You can't carry it around. But also it was a thing from childhood, something I wanted to leave behind. I wanted to get away, start working, become independent. And I didn't want to be bound at that stage by the obligation to practise. My life was not organised enough at that stage.'

As a teenager in Hastings she had liked Glam-rock acts like David Bowie. As a student at Brunel University studying nursing and social sciences – 'the boozer's degree' as she puts it – Jo moved on to moody singer-songwriters like Joni Mitchell, Bob Dylan and Leonard Cohen. After that she went through a phase of being a 'Goth' with plenty of gender-bending, black eye shadaw and purple lipstick. Leading Eighties' Goth rock exponents The Dammed are still one of Jo's favourite groups.

When Jo began performing as a stand-up comedian in 1986, she played the piano, performing topical comedy songs for, as she puts it, 'the purely pragmatic reason of padding out my performance. I didn't have enough material for a whole hour.'

RIGHT
Her Bach is worse than her bite. Jo reacts to a practice set-back.

Jo's musical journey

For the *Play it Again* challenge, Jo decided to take up the keyboard again, but this time in the form of the pipe organ. It has been a life-long ambition of hers to be able to play Bach's famous 'Toccata and Fugue', the signature tune of Hammer Horror-style organ music everywhere. More than that, she wanted to play the piece on a truly massive organ in a cathedral or classical concert hall.

'Having a go on an instrument like that – even for a few minutes – is an opportunity too good to miss ... a tremendous opportunity, once in a lifetime. It is going to be a huge thrill and I'm only going to get one shot at it.'

The appeal of the organ, Jo says, is in its drama: 'It's very Gothic, and I'm a bit of a Goth. There's the horror aspect. You can't hear it – especially the "Toccata" – without thinking of Vincent Price and all those completely over the top and un-scary Sixties horror films. And then there's the whole Terry Jones/Monty Python "And now for something completely different" element. And the whole Carry-On thing – "Oh missus, you've got a lovely big organ." You try to stay away from the double entendre, but it's completely impossible.'

Jo's previous musical training and her ability on the piano were a huge advantage in taking on the organ, but there was still much to learn. In addition to the familiar keyboard, Jo had to learn to play bass notes by operating the organ pedals with her feet. She found the pedals a big challenge to begin with. 'There's pain in the feet and ankles because you are not used to it, you have to rock your feet backwards and forwards with your ankles. It aches a lot and you can't do it for long.' Like a drummer, Jo needed to master the physical knack of co-ordinating all four limbs, timing them to work together and yet independently of each other. Playing the pedals is a bit like dancing.

The dexterity that Jo needed in her fingers has probably declined a bit with age. She had a fairly serious accident about 20 years ago when she crushed a finger under the runner of a sledge. The knuckle was broken and some flexibility was lost and as the 'Toccata and Fugue' involved moving her fingers quickly in repeated patterns, she could

RIGHT
Performing on the organ: a song in the heart, and a pain in the ankles.

'When you are nervous, your hands won't work in the way you want them to.'

have done without this particular injury. But her teacher, the conductor Hilary Davan Wetton, said her fingers were good enough, especially as she had no pain in either her fingers or arms. Nerves come into play, though. 'When you are nervous that's an added ingredient, it makes everything very difficult. Your hands won't work as you want them to.'

The other issue with the organ, as with the drums, is finding a place to practise. The best ones are built in churches (or cinemas and concert and dance halls) as part of the architecture. In fact, the interior of the church is actually part of the instrument – a resonating chamber like the body of a guitar or the bowl of a trumpet. Jo solved the problem by booking practice time at a local church but, mainly, by installing an electric organ in a shed in at the bottom of her back garden. With a bit of rudimentary soundproofing and by keeping the volume down, it was a practical arrangement with no complaints.

Going public

After a few lessons, Jo went back to the parish church in Benenden – the village where she had grown up – and accompanied the church choir on the organ. Jo felt less nervous playing with the choir because she knew that if she fluffed, they would cover up for her. In the event, Jo's performance was fine and it went much better than she had expected.

RIGHT
Jo entertains over a thousand guests at the Tower Ballroom, Blackpool.

Jo second challenge, however, was much more potentially harrowing. She agreed to play 'Ave Maria', accompanying an opera singer in a church during a friend's wedding. 'As a stage performer there's ways you can recover if you fluff it. You can always switch on the revolving bowtie – but with the organ you are completely vulnerable.

'At the wedding there wasn't anything else accompanying the singer and so there was nowhere to hide. I was terrified. I just kept concentrating on what I was playing and ignored the singer, praying that she would somehow stay in time. I was supposed to be accompanying her. But really she was accompanying me.'

'So far my most nerve-wracking comedy was at the Montreal Comedy Festival performing in front of 3,500 Canadians who don't always pick up on the English sense of humour. That was nightmarish.'

The final challenge

Jo's final challenge was to perform Bach's 'Toccata and Fugue' at a Christmas concert in front of a capacity 8,000 audience at the Royal Albert Hall. She prepared carefully and by the time of the concert she could play the piece fluently. But even for a seasoned performer like her, the idea of getting up on stage alone – without the support of a backing group or orchestra – was a little scary.

Jo was not worried about reading the music. It was the sheer effort required to control this enormous beast of an instrument and make it do what she wanted that was the problem. Just before she went on stage, her hands went cold and numb. It was a mild panic attack and worrying that her hands simply would not work made things worse.

In the event, Jo played the piece with only a couple of stumbles. More importantly, she played it in one go and received thunderous applause. It was a huge relief. Before the show she was concerned about how the classical audience might react. 'I'm really worried that the aficionados are going to find me out,' she had said. 'I have this nightmare vision of there being silence at the end of it before somebody shouts: "Bollocks!".' Fortunately, it transpired that the anticipation was far worse than the reality.

Chapter 4
Getting started

AGILE
GB

Setting your sights

The time and effort required to become a musical performer depends on your choice of instrument, your motivation and the targets you set for how well, or at what level, you want to play. At one end of the spectrum is the professional concert performer who may have practised for at least seven hours a day, every day since childhood. At the other end is learning the school recorder or an electronic sampler keyboard, both of which can be mastered comparatively quickly. In the middle is learning some classical favourites on the piano.

Learning the guitar in folk or rock style, which is massively popular, is on the easier side. Many of the folk and blues singers that Bill Oddie likes he learned to play using a famous Sixties book of music called *Play in a Day* by Bert Wheedon. The book still sells well, but there are now many other excellent music schemes and books available.

String, woodwind or brass instruments, on the other hand, can be more of a challenge – especially at first – and may take much more effort, particularly if you have wrongly judged your own aptitude for the instrument. With any of these instruments it is highly advisable to have formal lessons, even if it is only once a fortnight or once a month. The fact is, you need somebody to show you how to hold the instrument before you can get a note out of it (see opposite).

> 'It was great to have lessons from him, because he was so completely committed to the banjo. He inspired me.'
>
> FRANK SKINNER, PLAY IT AGAIN PARTICIPANT, ABOUT HIS TEACHER

Another factor is the quality of your instrument. For some instruments – especially the piano and guitar – it is very difficult indeed to learn on a bad quality instrument. For others, such as the violin, the quality of the instrument is not so important at the beginning (because you are not likely to sound wonderful at first in any case), but it becomes critical later on.

Whatever instrument you choose, there is a huge range of help available on the internet. There are entire automatic online lessons using the multimedia facilities of modern home computers and laptops to give simulated and interactive lessons (see pages 220–1).

Choosing a music teacher

As a rule of thumb, the more formal or classical your musical ambitions, the more teaching you will require. There's a healthy tradition of pop and rock guitarists teaching themselves, or swapping technique and ideas with other players. Here are some pointers to look out for.

* Make sure you choose a teacher who specialises in the type of music you want to play. Beyond the absolute basics, a classical clarinet teacher, for example, may not be the best person to choose if you want to specialise in jazz.
* Ask a potential teacher to put you in contact with existing pupils, as part of the process of deciding if the instrument as well as the teacher is right for you.
* Some teachers will emphasise their own ability or credentials as a professional player. Often teaching technique, patience and personality are more important, especially if you are a beginner.
* A 30-minute lesson should cost between £10 and £20; be prepared to double that when you progress to hour-long lessons. To begin with, it may be cheaper to take lessons in small groups, where the cost is shared.
* You might be interested in finding a Suzuki teacher. Here, group teaching is used as part of the revolutionary Suzuki method, originally developed for teaching very young children to play the (miniature) violin. The technique emphasises learning tunes by ear, with an element of trial and error, the ability to read music for a tune is often taught after it can be played by ear.

The guitar

The guitar is such a popular instrument that there are dozens of different varieties of instrument and many styles of playing. Here we are talking about the basic American-type acoustic guitar with steel strings, a circular sound hole and a relatively large body with a relatively narrow fret board. This type of guitar is the one used by the great singer-songwriters like Paul Simon and Bob Dylan and is the basic instrument of all folk rock and most pop music. It is played in a very different way to the classical or 'Spanish' guitar (nylon strings, wider fret board, smaller body) used in Flamenco and in classical music.

Buying strings

Most teachers recommend using relatively thin and soft ('light gauge' or 0.012 gauge) steel strings when you are learning. Even if they snap more easily than a heavier gauge, they are much kinder to your fingers. The thing that slows down most beginners is the sheer pain of pressing the strings with the fingertips. This is where lightweight strings help. The pain will go after a month or so of regular playing as (un-noticeable) layers of harder skin cover the sensitive areas.

The sound and playability of your guitar is affected by the type and quality of the strings. The wrong type or worn out strings will make even the best guitar in the world difficult to play and sound flat, just as even the best sports car in the world would be impossible to drive well with flat or worn tyres. It might not be sensible to buy an expensive professional brand of guitar like a Martin, for example, to begin with. But it does make sense to buy a few sets of Martin guitar strings and change them two or three times a year. You can buy sets of Martin or Fender light gauge strings on the internet for less than £10.

Getting under way

The great thing about the guitar is that it is possible to start making progress the moment you have tuned up the instrument for the first time. There is no need to learn to read music, at least in the early stages of mastering the instrument, and many folk, pop and rock guitarists never learn to read music, even professionals.

This is because, at beginner level in particular, the acoustic guitar is basically an accompanying instrument. Its role is to supply a strummed rhythm (which is sometimes 'finger-picked' – see page 140) and harmonising background chords. The tune is produced by the guitarist's voice or another instrument.

Chords can be written out 'long hand' as a series of notes stacked one on top of each other. You may have seen notation like that in music written for the piano, where it tells a pianist to play these notes all at the same time, producing a harmonising chord, like voices blending together in a choir. Chords and melodies for the guitar can be written in the same way, but they are more often written in tablature (tab) form – little diagrams identifying the name of the chord (for example, D major is known as 'D'; D minor as 'Dm') and showing exactly where each finger should be placed on each string (see opposite).

No special training is needed to be able to read tabs. You look at the pattern for any particular chord, place your fingers on the fret board, press down hard, strum with the other hand and, with a little effort to begin with, 'read' the tab, changing notation into music. The disadvantage with tab notation, as opposed to reading traditional music notation, is that it is preferable to know the tune in advance both to strum with the right rhythm and to know when to change the chord. The tabs can also be difficult to read at speed, so it is best to learn the tabs and then play the music from memory.

Re-stringing and tuning a guitar

Re-stringing involves removing all the existing strings, replacing them in the right order and then tightening the strings until the instrument is in tune. Tuning is something that not only needs doing when you have new strings, but checking the tuning is a ritual you go through each time you pick up the guitar and even when playing it. Relative tuning from a tuning fork (or any other single-tone source) is a time-consuming process for a beginner and it requires a good ear, although all that training of pitch perception develops the musical ear very effectively. It is as much a part of the learning process as the fingering of notes and chords.

Tuning pipes (a sort of small harmonica that plays each required note in turn) or a small, hand-held electronic tone generator (they cost about £15 in music shops) can be used if you don't have access to a piano and find relative tuning difficult.

There is also a lot of help available on the internet. There are numerous sites that play the tones for each correctly tuned open string of the guitar (for example, at www.8notes.com/guitar_tuner). Tighten each string very slowly until it exactly matches the tone on the site, making sure that the tone you have matched is the right one, and not an octave above or below the required note.

Reading guitar chord charts and tabs

There are three ways in which guitar chords and melodies are written:

Guitar chord chart: the chord of D

On this chart, the strings are the vertical lines and the frets are the horizontal lines. The dots show where your fingers should go. Zero means play an open string and an 'X' means do not play that string. Some charts use numbers to tell you which finger to place on each string.

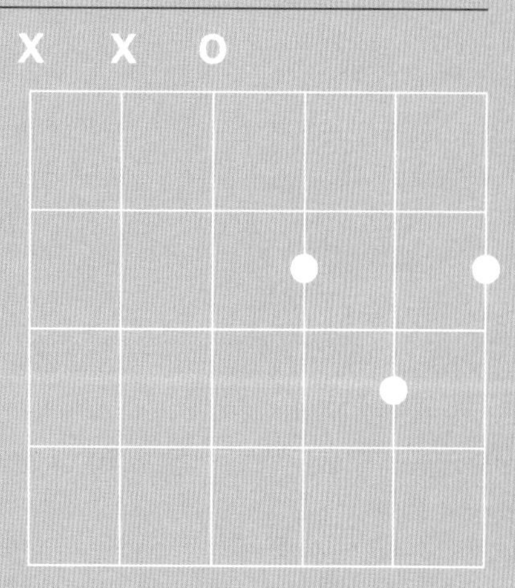

Guitar tab for chords: the chord of D

The rows represent each string and the numbers tell you which fret to hold the string down on.

```
e |--- 2---
B |--- 3---
G |--- 2---
D |--- 0---
A |--- X---
E |--- X---
       D
```

Guitar tab for melodies: excerpt from 'Twinkle, Twinkle, Little Star'

The numbers here represent which fret of which string you put your fingers on – here, only the G and D strings are used. As with all tabs, it does not show the tempo and exact rhythm.

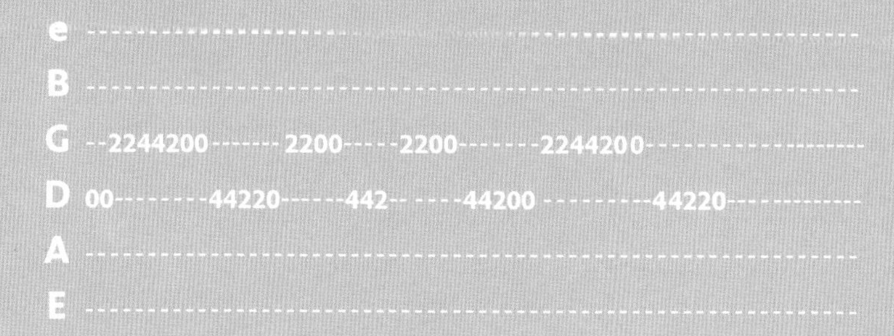

SPIDER

There are thousands – perhaps millions – of web pages displaying tab music written by guitarists and fans who have worked out how to play along with a particular song, and then noted down the chord patterns as tabs. It is pretty certain that you will be able to find the tabs for any song you care to think of at the click of a mouse (usually on a page with all kinds of technical tips on how to form the chords, shortcuts, simple variations and so on).

Sheet music usually includes both staff notation and the tabs. An ability to read the melodic line in the treble clef of traditional music (see page 150) is useful for an intermediate guitarist who wants to pick out the tune (as opposed to just strumming the chords) in order to play a solo, or to play lead guitar in a group. But even this is not strictly necessary.

Solo guitar music is also often written out as a tab (see the third example on page 137). Many of the famous fast-paced virtuoso guitar 'licks' and 'riffs' beloved of blues, rock and heavy metal electric guitarists are noted in this way. Electric guitar solos may need skill and practice, but the ability to read music is not necessarily a requirement and an inability to read music will not slow you down.

Of course, it might help to be able to read and write music in order to compose songs, but in practice, many pop and folk song composers work 'by ear', recording their compositions electronically. Voice-recognition computer programmes will then translate music played into a microphone into perfect musical notation (see page 221).

From small beginnings

Most pop songs can be accompanied with just three simple chords related to the key that the song is in. For example, if the song is in G major, then you could accompany it with the chords for G major, C major and D major. Most people would be able to master that in the single (full-time, eight-hour) day mentioned in the title of Mr Wheedon's famous *Play in a Day* system. More realistically, you would be able to do it after practising regularly (for as long as your fingers will let you) for a week.

Thereafter, the business of learning to play the guitar as a rhythmic accompanying instrument is mainly a matter of memorising and practising more and more guitar chords – or 'shapes' – learned from tab diagrams. Add a minor chord, such as the simple A minor shape, and this will add a more dramatic, darker tone.

The weakness and lack of dexterity in the left hand can be frustrating at first. If you have normal levels of finger dexterity, you will at first find it difficult to move your fingers quickly from one pattern to another, experiencing a feeling of being 'all fingers and thumbs'. Like the slight discomfort in the fingertips, this problem should pass quickly – unlike the problem of tone deafness, all the expert agree that dexterity improves markedly with practice. Once you have mastered a dozen or so chords, you will be able to strum along to almost any song played on mainstream radio and topping the download charts (well, at least parts of it).

Strumming and finger-picking

Simple **strumming** is fine for beginners, but it can start to sound a bit monotonous after a while. More complex strumming styles – different rhythm patterns – can be learned, copying the style of individual players, or types of playing, whether these are different folk styles or reggae, or different pop and dance rhythms. As with chords and tabs, there are huge numbers of pages on the web devoted to strumming and rhythm styles for guitarists.

Eventually, you will feel confident enough to start 'plucking' or '**picking**' more in the style of a harp or classical guitar instead of strumming. Picking means applying each finger to a separate string and plucking each in turn according to a particular pattern or 'picking style'. Sometimes this style is called 'claw picking' because the fingers are arched like a chicken claw, pulling and plucking at the strings all at the same time or one by one.

Finger picking requires a lot more co-ordination between the hands, but it does allow you to play melody as well as harmonising chords. The most advanced picking styles are associated with Irish folk music and American bluegrass and country music. A finger-picked guitar played in ensemble with a banjo and a violin creates one of the most distinctive and impressive sounds in acoustic popular and folk music.

Playing rhythm guitar

Electric rhythm guitar playing is essentially just an amplified version of the sort of acoustic guitar playing described above. There are specialised semi-acoustic electric guitars (see page 92), but rhythm style can be played on the more common solid bodied 'lead' electric guitar by adjusting its tone controls. If you are already confident playing on the acoustic guitar, you should have little difficulty in taking up the rhythm guitar and playing along with others in a group.

Electric rhythm guitar playing requires further practice of advanced picking and the mastery of more off-beat strumming styles (for example, in reggae). The player also has to learn how to transpose the basic 'open' chords described in most tab diagrams into 'barre' chords, which are played higher up the neck, producing the crisper and more percussive sound that works best with amplified electronic music.

Playing lead guitar

'Lead guitar' is a style of playing that emphasises the picking out of melody – strings of individual notes – rather than the playing of full chords. The lead can either carry the tune of the song, replacing the voice or, more commonly, play counter melodies and 'riffs' that respond to the voice, filling it out or giving it an extra catchy hook. A competent electric guitarist will easily be able to switch between rhythm and lead guitar playing – the two styles influenced the line-up of the modern rock band. The 'classic' rock and roll group (such as the Beatles) consisted of elaborations on the theme of drums, bass guitar and two electric guitars – one played in the rhythm style and the other played as a lead guitar.

Most of the famous electric rock and blues players – Jimi Hendrix, Eric Clapton, Carlos Santana, Frank Zappa and Jimmy Page, among others – played lead guitar. Their fame was based on exploring the (at the time new and revolutionary) electronic sound possibilities of their instruments and on their ability to play long, rapid runs of notes in the style of great modern jazz saxophonists like John Coltrane. Lead guitar playing is largely a matter of learning how to play these runs of notes.

'At some point, it's like a communion of some kind. We get connected to ourselves by music.'

ERIC CLAPTON, GUITARIST

As with chord patterns, many of these riffs have been written down in diagrammatic form and made available over the internet. Depending on how good your hand-eye co-ordination is, and your level of dexterity, it can take anything from days to years to master the more difficult ones.

Electric lead guitarists tend to collect riffs and licks in the same way that acoustic and rhythm players collect and swap chord patterns. And because many of these riffs were originally improvisations and never written down in proper notation to begin with, they can be adapted, developed or merged into other riffs each time they are played.

Playing the bass guitar

The difference between the electric guitar and bass guitar is that it has only four strings and these are rarely played together to produce chords. Instead notes are played one by one. The role of the bass player in a group is normally to emphasise the base note of chords that are being played by other group members on the piano or guitar.

At a more advanced level, bassists produce 'stepping' runs of notes leading the group from one chord to another. Experienced bass players may also play solos or even carry the melodic lead of a song, or at least part of it.

Playing the banjo

There are many similarities between folk guitar and banjo playing. The main difference, however, is that the banjo is plucked (or 'finger-picked') with the right hand instead of strummed. This makes right-hand technique on the banjo harder to master than the guitar, but the fingering of the neck by the left hand is simpler and correspondingly easier.

Banjos were once strummed. The instrument had an important role in providing strummed rhythm and droning harmony in early forms of jazz. By the 1930s, however, the banjo had been replaced in jazz and dance bands by the tightly-strung f-hole rhythm guitar. It was then played mainly as a folk tradition in the rural American south, where it became a mainstay of a specialised form of fast 'hillbilly' music called bluegrass. The less common four-stringed tenor banjo had developed in Ireland, where it is still an important folk instrument.

Banjo playing revived in the 1960s as part of the same American folk music boom that also spread the popularity of the guitar. The Sixties revival was associated with the folk singer Pete Seeger, whose book *How to Play the Five String Banjo*, is still popular.

Music for the banjo is mostly written in tab form and most learning is by ear, which simply involves listening to the banjo part in a piece of bluegrass and then copying it with the help of tab diagrams. 'Jamming' with other bluegrass players is more important than formal lessons, since there's a tradition of players swapping tips about technique. There are also dozens of fan sites on the internet offering tabs for bluegrass tunes (for example, at www.bluegrassworld.com).

> 'I just want to play my banjo. I want to sing and dance until I die. Play my banjo ...'
>
> BILLY CONNOLLY, COMEDIAN

The circular motion of banjo finger-picking – the patterns are known as 'rolls' (and some patterns are named after famous players who invented them) – looks like a person drumming their fingers in an irritated way on a tabletop, one finger after the next in a quick, but smooth and continuous, motion. Learning a good range of right-hand rolls and picking styles is key to progressing on the banjo. As with tabs, players traditionally share patterns, rolls and styles, which are then learned, adapted, hybridised and passed on as you might learn dance steps.

Most experienced banjo players add 'picks', which look like long, artificial metal or plastic fingernails, to the tips of the fingers of their right hand to add volume and additional trademark 'crispiness' to the sound.

The piano

Formal musical education in this country is largely based around the idea of playing the piano. At the level of university music courses and specialist colleges there is usually an assumption that people playing any instrument – even in jazz and pop styles – also have some sort of proficiency at the piano.

The whole business of reading and writing music is also wrapped up with piano playing. Our idea of a 'proper musician' is somebody who, like the music teacher we all had at school, picks up a book of sheet music, places it on the piano, blinks at it and then begins to play. But this is not the only way.

Teach yourself chord accompaniments

You can learn to play the piano 'by ear' as an accompanying instrument to your own singing (or that of others) or as a rhythm instrument in a group quite quickly. And, as in the case of the guitar, you can do this with only very limited knowledge of musical theory or ability to read music.

Playing 'by ear' – as also with the guitar – means essentially playing chord patterns. And while the fingering for piano chords is not normally set out as guitar-type tabs (see page 137), there are books of diagrammatic piano chords showing where to place your fingers to produce particular note combinations, without reference to musical notation. Make things even easier for yourself by using an electronic keyboard with built-in tutorial programming (see page 148).

> 'Playing the piano changes your state of mind and blots out all your worries.'
>
> DIANE ABBOTT, PLAY IT AGAIN PARTICIPANT

Even better, there are numerous free sites on the internet uploaded by enthusiasts showing how to finger any particular chord you want to play. One such site is the Chord House at www.looknohands.com/chordhouse/piano/. If you know the name of the chord you want to play, enter it on the screen and you both hear it and see it as a diagram, showing you where you need to put your fingers on the keyboard to play it.

So if you wanted to play, for example, a famous piano-based pop song like Elton John's 'Candle In The Wind', you simply look up the chords for the song on a tabs site, note the chords you will need, learn the fingering for each one by using a Chord House-type site and then accompany yourself with three- or four-finger piano chords. Some sites (such as at www.e-chords.com/) offer both guitar and piano chord diagrams to hundreds of mainstream pop songs.

At first, it's best to play the same chord shape with both hands, perhaps alternating the left and right hands to create a rhythm – eventually you can introduce a bit of melody or 'riff' playing with the right hand.

Many pop musicians mastered the piano in this way – a classic example is Paul McCartney. He started by playing rhythm guitar, switched to bass guitar and then on to the piano where, at first, he simply transposed his knowledge of guitar chords to the keyboard and accompanied his own singing in the same way.

Playing the electronic keyboard

Electronic keyboards are ideal instruments for beginners, to be played alongside the traditional acoustic piano or in their own right. One advantage is that a keyboard can be played and practised silently using headphones to listen to the electronically synthesised notes.

Full-size keyboards are readily available using a system of lights to show you where to put your fingers to produce particular chords, melodic patterns or even whole songs and simple classical pieces and, for good measure, showing you the notation on a small screen if you are interested in learning to read music. Some versions even monitor your playing, sounding warnings when you make errors and giving grades for accuracy of playing.

Most keyboards like this come with hundreds of songs and tunes pre-programmed so that you can play just parts of them (for example, concentrating on developing your right hand melody playing while the keyboard sympathetically plays the left hand part) to begin with.

Most interestingly of all, electronic keyboards can now be very easily connected to computers and, therefore, to the internet to search for new sheet music and other teaching resources and even to network with remote keyboard players for ensemble playing.

Taking formal piano lessons

For every pianist who enjoys playing chords to accompany themselves or others with pop and rock songs, there are those who learn to play in a more conventional way by taking lessons with a teacher. You will find that many instrumental teachers particularly enjoy teaching adults because they come to their lessons with a different perspective. Furthermore, don't be afraid that you will be playing from childish music books, there are plenty of collections of music out there aimed at the adult learner.

Reading music

The treble clef

This clef is used to write music for instruments that play higher pitched notes, such as the violin, flute and trumpet. The set of five parallel lines that all music is written on is called a staff and notes are written either on the lines or in the spaces between them. Each note has a name – A, B, C, D, E, F or G (which are repeated) – and the higher their position on the staff, the higher is their pitch.

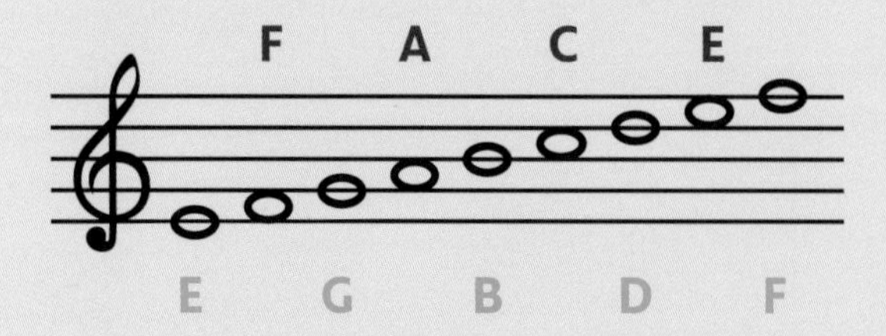

The bass clef

This clef is used to write music for instruments that play lower pitched notes, such as the cello and bassoon. Some instruments will use both this and the treble clef either separately, as for the cello, or together, in the case of the piano. There are several other clefs, but the treble and the bass are the most commonly used ones.

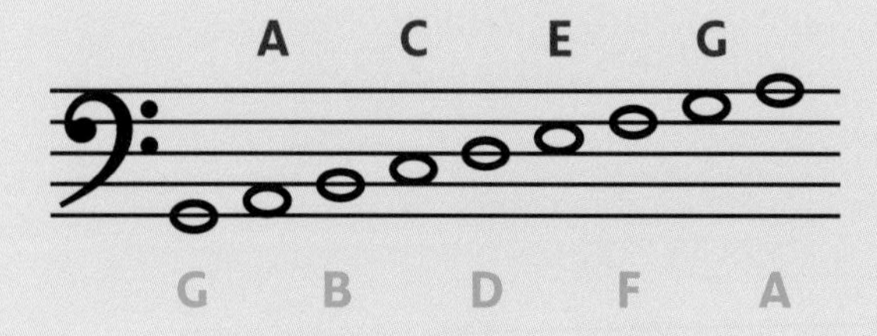

Note duration

Different shapes of note denote different lengths of time. Here, the first note – called a crotchet – has a value of one beat. The next is a minim, which is worth two beats, and the third is a semibreve, worth four beats. There are many other durations, some longer, some shorter.

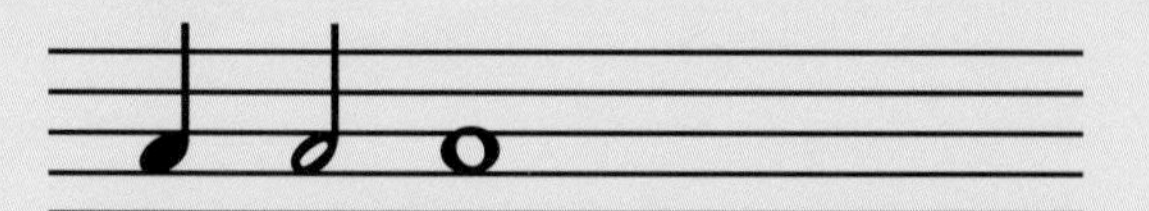

Other symbols

As you learn to read music, so you come across new symbols. Here are a few of the most commonplace:

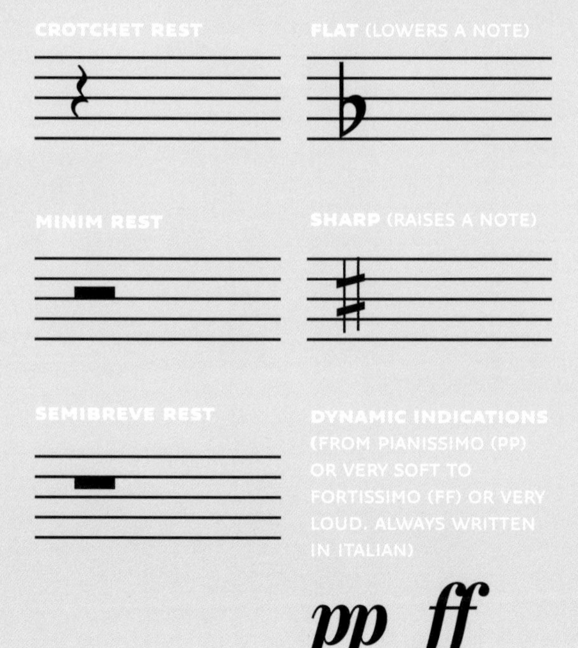

At first it may seem that your fingers are stiff and uncoordinated, but given time and practice, you'll be delving into whatever musical genre most appeals. Every time you overcome a new hurdle – playing with both hands separately, playing with both hands together, playing a piece that contains more than five notes, playing your first simple piece by a well-known composer – there is an incredible sense of achievement that encourages you on to the next step.

Learning to read music

Written music can look intimidating, but it is, in fact, a logical way of setting out how a composition is to be played. Learning to read music is an important part of learning to play most instruments – guitar tabs (see page 137) are a form of music script and traditional notation on a staff (the parallel lines on which the notes are written – see opposite) is merely a different form of music script. Even if a musician can eventually play their pieces without looking at their music, this is more a feat of memory than having learnt the music 'by ear'. ❚

What music tells you

Even for the simplest of pieces, being able to read music enables a musician to know, among other things:

- How fast or slow the music should be played.
- What notes to play – whether for a single line in the case of, say, flute or trumpet, or something more complex for, say, the piano.
- Whether to play loud or soft or somewhere in between.
- What rhythms are involved.

As with the process of learning the instrument itself, learning to read music is a matter of mastering a few easy basic foundations and building on that with patience, practice and growing confidence – see the page opposite.

The violin

On the violin, the player has to physically produce each note and a lot of practice in the early stages is aimed at producing a clean sound. You definitely need to need to consult a teacher, or an existing player, to show you how to stand or sit when playing the instrument and, equally importantly, how to hold the bow and move it across the strings.

Most beginning players apply far too much pressure when bowing. The aim is to pull the bow across the strings with a delicate motion, coaxing the notes gently from the instrument. Although developing a good bow technique may take a while, poor technique is no barrier to playing the instrument – after a fashion – or to learning how to finger the instrument. As with bowing, you need to develop a smooth and accurate fingering technique. Since the finger positions are not fixed on the fingerboard, very few beginners can play accurately enough so that each note is perfectly in tune.

> 'Always in my playing I strive to surpass myself, and it is this constant struggle that makes music fascinating to me.'
>
> JASCHA HEIFETZ, VIOLINIST

The result – especially when combined with poor bow technique – can often sound pretty awful. Beginners can just slightly miss each note, playing each one slightly sharp or flat, creating an effect similar to a singer with very poor pitch discrimination. To help overcome this potentially ghastly combination, teachers of string instruments tend to start with using pizzicato (plucking at the strings with the right hand) for playing notes that are fingered and just using the bow on open strings – where no fingers are used. Only when the player is confident with the ability of both left and right hands are the two put together.

When learning to play the violin, press on regardless, even if the sound is not so good. As with any instrument, the more you play, the better it will sound. Progress can be very rapid in mastering a sweeter tone as finger dexterity improves. Likewise, playing in tune improves naturally, as the relative positions needed for the fingers becomes a habit, embedded in the physical 'muscle memory'.

The clarinet or saxophone

The clarinet and saxophone are solo instruments, designed to carry the lead melody, like a singer in a group, or supply harmony, like a member of a choir or vocal harmony group. Learning these instruments, then, does not make a great deal of sense unless you plan to play in a group or ensemble or, at the very least, play along with a pianist or an electronic backing track. One difference between the clarinet and the saxophone is that the former is mainly used in classical music, with (these days) a small role in jazz or pop music. The saxophone is mainly a jazz instrument, also widely used in pop, but with only a limited role in classical music.

Because of this, it is important to be able to learn to read music, so you can fit in with others reading from the same score. You will also definitely need to have some formal lessons when tackling either of these instruments.

> 'Music is your own experience, your own thoughts, your wisdom. If you don't live it, it won't come out of your horn.'
>
> CHARLIE PARKER, JAZZ SAXOPHONIST

The sound of the saxophone is rougher than the clarinet, and so it easier to get that right at first. The sax tends to be played with softer reeds, which resonate more easily, so the tone is less precise and crisp than that of the clarinet. This gives the clarinet the edge in playing very subtle and delicate solos, but it also makes the clarinet that much harder to play than the sax for beginners. People who start on sax rather than clarinet tend to progress much faster in the early stages.

Another advantage of learning the alto saxophone for beginners who played recorder at school is that the fingering, except for the addition of extra keys to produce sharps and flats, is exactly the same as a recorder – at least, to begin with. A flautist, saxophonist and clarinettist each have to learn different positions for the same notes in different octaves – some 82 different fingering positions. Because of this – and because of the different embouchure demanded by the clarinet – it is easier for a clarinettist to master the saxophone. If you start on the saxophone, you will, however, find it more difficult to move on to the clarinet.

The flute

Progress on the flute depends very largely on the aptitude you have for producing a clean tone by blowing correctly over the embouchure hole. You need to make sure that you can do this before you decide to take up the instrument. Even if your embouchure technique is good, it may take time before you can produce a clean sound easily and consistently. At the start, playing the flute is physically taxing – the muscles of the face can ache and some people can even become dizzy from blowing too hard (a very common beginner's error).

Unlike the piano or guitar, you will not be able to get a single note out of the instrument until you can blow correctly. It is therefore very important to get a teacher or, at the least, an experienced player, to show you how to hold the instrument and how to blow correctly. There are books and online diagrams showing you how to do this, but this is a case where you need an experienced person to show you exactly where to put your fingers, what is the correct posture, and how to angle your head and mouth relative to the instrument.

The particular physical demands of the instrument will limit practice time to begin with. As well as correct blowing into the flute, you will need to develop your breathing capacity, which is related to diaphragm control. The key is to play 'little and often' – several sessions of a few minutes each day would be ideal to begin with. Once the blowing technique is there, it will be easier to make practice sessions longer and therefore get more out of formal lessons.

After this initial hurdle is overcome, progress may come quickly. The fingering method is simple and – unlike the violin or trumpet, for example – a beginner sounds perfectly tuneful.

Making progress

For any instrument, the key to progress is to schedule in regular practice times. With a 30-minute weekly lesson followed up by two or three half-hour practice sessions, you will soon make progress. It will be even quicker if you are able to pick up the instrument in odd minutes in between, or entertain yourself by playing along with snippets from favourite classical or pop pieces.

The trumpet

Brass instruments are generally easier to play than most other classical or orchestral instruments. But there are difficulties. As with woodwind instruments, the key is developing a good blowing technique. You may find that the process of producing a clean note using a mouthpiece is too difficult or unpleasant, but if you find you can produce a note relatively easily, early practice should all be about improving blowing technique. Fingering – which is very simple on a trumpet – comes later.

Ask a teacher to show you how to breathe properly and hold air in your mouth. Most beginners tend to hold too much air and attempt to force this through the mouthpiece, just as you might do when blowing a balloon. Puffing out your cheeks like this is exhausting. In the longer term, it might even result in the sort of bulging, baggy cheeks developed by Dizzy Gillespie. The jazz trumpet legend had his own unique sound, but most teachers would be horrified by his technique – it was completely wrong!

> 'The music is important because it's an art form that takes in the mythology of our people.'
>
> WYNTON MARSALIS, JAZZ TRUMPETER AND COMPOSER

Even if you find yourself able to produce a solid sound from the mouthpiece, you may find the process of producing the notes a little uncomfortable to begin with. Initially, you may find that your lips go slightly numb and that you experience an unpleasant metallic taste. Similarly, the vibration of the lips against metal caused by the necessary 'raspberry' action needed to play the instrument can cause an alarming tingling sensation. These effects will go away shortly after a practice session and, as you improve, they will go away altogether, and the whole process of making the notes will seem natural and comfortable.

Early practice is all about getting the right posture and perfecting breathing and blowing technique. The aim then is to become accomplished in holding a steady note and accurately controlling pitch without using the valves. Once this process is under control – it's the equivalent of learning to bow a string instrument correctly, or a guitarist developing hardened skin and the ability to press strings against the fret board – you can progress quickly to playing tunes and scales. A vast amount of simple solo and band music exists for the trumpet and other brass instruments. ▌

The drums

The standard drum kit is a relatively easy instrument to master if you have good gross motor skills and dexterity. The key to the drums is an ability to move both hands and both feet independently and in sequences and patterns that make up rhythms or standard beats or grooves.

The left foot operates a pedal, which controls a large drumstick, causing it to pound against the large bass drum. The right foot operates a second pedal, which causes two treble cymbals – the hi-hat – to crash together. Other cymbals, the hi-hat itself, an upward-facing snare drum and one or more upward-facing tom-tom drums, are struck with a pair of thin drumsticks, one stick in each hand.

> 'I played with everyone; people who were better than me and it made me improve.'
>
> CHAD SMITH, DRUMMER, RED HOT CHILI PEPPERS

Most people find they can tap out a simple alternating beat with the drumsticks straight away. With regular practice, most people ought to be able to use the foot pedals as well as the sticks to beat out the sort of simple rhythm patterns found in, for example, heavy rock music. After that it is a matter of memorising different sequences on the pedals and with the sticks corresponding to different standard beats – blues, bossa nova, hi life, disco, reggae, and so on.

With practice, a beginner could aim to be fluent in all standard patterns within a year. At some point, the 'beats' become second nature – like knowing the steps to various ballroom or modern dance routines. After that, the drummer can concentrate on varying the basic beats, adding drum rolls and 'fill' patterns, which are studied and collected by listening to recordings of great players.

It is not necessary to learn to read music to play the drums or to have lessons from an expert teacher. It might be an idea, though, to persuade or hire somebody who already plays drums to show you how to set up the kit, tune the skins and hold the sticks. After that, the lessons available online at a vast number of drumming websites will probably be enough to get you going. As with any pop, rock or jazz instrument, it really helps to practise by playing along to recordings of tunes you like or – to begin with – easy play-along pieces for drummers.

Music exams

If you decide that you want a more formal and structured approach to playing an instrument, you need to look into the system of grade exams supervised by the Associated Board of the Royal Schools of Music (ABRSM) at www.abrsm.org or Trinity Guildhall at www.trinitycollege.co.uk.

The grades system is based on the assumption that a person with average aptitude, who practises for half an hour, three or four days a week, will take between one and two years to pass through each grade (there are eight grades in all). For older players, it might be worth taking the ABRSM's performance assessment for adults, which provides a measure of aptitude and a guide to just how much effort will be needed to become a competent classical or jazz player. The test highlights any problems with aptitude and it can be taken again to measure progress, as an alternative to taking the more formal grade exams. As well as exams based on classical music, the ABRSM offers a jazz syllabus for piano and other instruments and Trinity Guildhall offers 'Rockschool' graded exams for electric guitar, drums, bass guitar, vocals and popular piano.

> 'Over 620,000 candidates take our music exams each year in more than 90 countries.'
>
> THE ASSOCIATED BOARD OF THE ROYAL SCHOOLS OF MUSIC

Grade one

At grade one you can sight-read and play basic major chords and scales as well as understanding the meaning of all common musical symbols, time signatures and the terminology used on musical scores.

To pass the exam you would have to play three pieces from a wide choice together with some scales, sight-reading and aural tests. A typical grade one piece recently set in an exam is Mozart's 'Allegro in F' – a simple piece first written for the harpsichord, and sounding a bit like a music box when played. To get an idea of the standard at grade one you can listen to this piece online at one of several dedicated Mozart 'midi' sites (midi files play tunes using non-polyphonic tones, a bit like old-fashioned mobile phone ring-tones). This tune is available, for example, at a Japanese Mozart fan site at http://windy.vis.ne.jp/art/datahall/mozart.htm. On the grade one jazz syllabus for piano, a recent exam piece is 'Oh Lord Don't Let Them Drop That Atomic Bomb On Me' by Charles Mingus. You can hear a midi version of this tune at www.last.fm/music/Charles+Mingus. Alternatively, the exam boards sell CDs containing all the pieces at each grade, which sound much more attractive than midi files as they reproduce the actual sound of the instrument.

Grades two and three

After a few years, you will obviously be a far more versatile player, able to play music from a wider range of genres. To get a taste of the standard of music for the grade three piano exam, listen to the 'Vivace' from *Sonatina in B flat* by Wesley (available at http://myweb.tiscali.co.uk/claypiano/midis.htm). The three pieces chosen for each exam are from a wide variety of styles, ranging from early Baroque through to the most contemporary of compositions. You don't have to do all the exams; it is perfectly acceptable to miss out an exam or two if you are moving on at speed.

Grades four and above

You can get an idea of grade four standard on the piano by listening to Handel's 'Allemande'. A midi is available at a specialised classical midi site at www.classicalmidiconnection.com/cmc/handel.html. Grades five, six and seven are progressively more difficult.

The jazz exams stop at grade five. For an example of the standard of jazz playing at this grade, listen to the piano parts on Bill Strayhorn's 'Take The A-Train'. You can download a free MP3 of the tune, or listen to it on the web at www.ez-tracks.com/getsong-songid-11485.html. As well as playing their pieces, the examinees are also expected to improvise on the main theme as part of each grade, becoming progressively more complex.

If a player wants to go beyond grade five with the ABRSM exams, then a music theory exam has to be taken. This is the only theory exam that is mandatory. If you take the Trinity Guildhall exams, no theory exam has to be taken.

Grade eight

In order to pass at grade eight, the student has to be able to play from memory just about any possible chord or scale nominated by the examiner using a complete range of rhythmic styles and arpeggios. In addition, she or he will also play for the examiner three difficult and lengthy pieces. To give you an idea of the standard that is achieved for a pianist, the examinee could play one of the trickier Bach 'Preludes and Fugues', a movement from a Mozart or Beethoven piano sonata and a piece by a major 20th-century composer, such as Copland or Gershwin.The grade eight exam is a ferocious beast, effectively the moment of fate for anyone aiming for a career in professional music. ❚

VIC FIRTH
'The drums are at the centre of everything, driving the group ... the whole performance.'

Aled Jones plays rock drums

Aled Jones is one of Britain's most successful professional musical performers. He shot to fame as a child with his flawless singing of 'Walking In The Air', the timeless Christmas classic from *The Snowman*. More recently he has become a television presenter and personality, making a big name for himself as a contestant on the BBC's *Strictly Come Dancing*, while singing, managing a group and releasing records.

Aled was born in 1970 in Llandegfan, Anglesey. His first public performance was in a local parish hall when he was at primary school. He played the part of Joseph in a nativity play, and discovered a natural talent for singing and performing. Aled soon started winning several national singing competitions and at the Eisteddfodau (annual Welsh festivals of literature, music and performance), and in 1979, he won first prize there – a huge honour in the Welsh-speaking and international musical world.

LEFT
Aled is already a master of melody. Now he's switching to rhythm: 'It's a completely different approach.'

A July 1985 BBC issue of his rendition of Andrew Lloyd-Webber's 'Memory' was something of a flop. But the follow-up – 'Walking In The Air' – was a complete triumph. The song was a smash hit and made Aled an international star. Since then, he's been a regular presenter on *Songs of Praise* (where he also sings) and also presented his own chat show on Radio Wales and a talent show on S4C.

Aled's musical journey

By the time Aled took on the *Play it Again* challenge he had been signed up to do even more TV presenting. It meant that time for practising an entirely new instrument would be hard to find, but, undeterred, he set himself the challenge of playing the drums. 'I have always been at the front of the stage,' he said. 'It has always been me out there with a band or an orchestra behind me. That was great. But it will be nice to be at the back, driving something forward, looking at performance in an entirely different way.'

There was another difference. Aled was plunging into the world of rock – basing his style on John Bonham, the legendary former Led Zeppelin drummer famous for his relentless, heavy, pounding sound. In musical terms, it's about as far away from his beginning as a cathedral choir boy as it is possible to get.

Aled's tutor, Erik Stams, who teaches at the drum and percussion school Drumtech, set Aled the challenge of playing drums in a Led Zeppelin tribute group in front of a crowd of expert rock fans, ready to pounce on the slightest error. It meant he would have to learn to play as well as John Bonham, often hailed as the greatest drummer in the history of heavy rock. And he would have to do that in just a few months.

Aled felt the pressure straight away. 'If I screw up as a singer,' he said, 'then I can cover up and maybe the orchestra and band can compensate for me. I can hide it. I forget words all the time on stage. I can recover. But with the drums, you can't. You are driving the entire performance.'

Aled spent most of his practice time using a set of drum practice pads. They have the same surface as an authentic drum kit, but they are flat and don't resonate. Pads allow the learner to practise technique without annoying the neighbours. 'The first thing you have to think of with drums,' he says, 'is the neighbours. You really need to sort out how you are going to practise. The pads are a good idea, but it only really comes together when you play the full kit. You can't really progress without that.

'Practising on the pads is a bit like learning scales – it's a means to an end. Every lesson starts with doing work on pads. The teacher demonstrates and then you copy and then you move on to the kit itself, hopefully to learn something new. Then you start building up – the patterns go into your body – you wouldn't be able to get your body to play the instrument without hours on the pads.

'You have to learn scales on the pads so that your fingers can move in a particular way. This is the same, except it's your whole body and not just fingers.' Even with his practice arrangements under control – and access to the best quality equipment and teaching – Aled struggled. First of all, although he could read music this didn't help him all that much. Drum patterns are written in a form of notation all of their own, so there was a new set of symbols and rules to learn.

'If my teacher writes something down in musical notation, I can get that,' Aled says. 'But the difficult thing is getting my body to do it. It's not like learning one musical instrument, you're learning a whole lot of them at the same time: snare drum, cymbals, big bass drum, hi-hat, tom-toms, the lot. You have to get on top of each of them and that's just the start – the easy bit. You've then got to get them all working together.

'You have to have four brains, one to control each limb, getting them all playing independently. It's harder than it looks. Co-ordination – that's been a big challenge, but I think I'm OK. I will get there if I can practise enough.'

In his first lesson, Aled learnt a simple BOOM – BAH – BA BOOM-BOOM – BAH on the bass drum, played with a foot pedal, and the snare drum, played with a drumstick. Not too difficult that – only two brains needed. That was a

RIGHT
Think of the neighbours. You can minimise the noise, but you'll still need a place to practise.

warm-up routine, using a simple and near universal 4/4 rock beat, which was a favourite of John Bonham's. Getting that right, Aled found, was the key to doing more complex and impressive stuff. It was like laying down a foundation.

'That beat was a very simple Led Zeppelin thing. But what's been amazing is seeing what you can build on that – there's just so many styles, so many intricacies with the drums, which I never realised before.

'Everyone says it is easy to play the drums. That's true in a way. It is easy to play 1-2, 1-2 – that's easy, it's second nature. But try putting a second beat on that, so it becomes 1-2, 1-4, 1-2, 1-4.'

Aled found that he had to work hard at learning more complex rhythms, because his body was just too used to going 1-2, 1-2 all the time, like the rhythm of walking or marching. 'Drumming is more like dancing. The rhythms and getting them right can drive you mad. You need to learn the patterns, get your body working, get your body doing what your mind wants it to do.'

RIGHT
Aled having a good time performing at the Camden Rock Café.

Going public

After about 10 one-hour lessons, and as much practice in between as he could manage, Aled was ready for his first TV challenge. He had to play along to a Lenny Kravitz song in front of an audience of fellow Drumtech students. 'The students had been playing drums for a couple of years,' Aled said proudly, 'they were ahead of me. But I was OK. I was fine with them and I passed the test – just about – which was an achievement. It was scary playing in front of other people, but exhilarating as well. It was then that I thought, "Yeah, I like this. I'm going to stay with this. I want to be really good at it".'

Which was just as well. The gig with the Led Zeppelin group was now only a few weeks away. Aled warmed up with a few more minor gigs and a masterclass from Stuart Copeland, the former drummer with The Police. Copeland was impressed with Aled's progress but, at the same time, warned him: 'Don't give up the day job.'

The gig itself took place at the appropriately grungey Camden Rock Café in London, in front of a packed crowd

'It's very physical.
You have to play drums
with your whole body.'

of 200–300 heavy metal fans. The scene was dark, hot, crowded and sweaty – lots of leather jackets and motorbike types. At first, the signs were not good. Before the band came on, the crowd started jeering and sarcastically chanting 'Walking In The Air'. Tough audience. These people knew every note and beat of every Led Zeppelin tune. They were tanked up and unlikely to look kindly on any fluffs.

As part of the act, all the group put on wigs, so they looked like 1970s' heavy metal rockers. At this point Aled freaked out – ever so slightly. He was nervous enough about going on stage, but he drew the line at wearing a fake moustache and wig designed to make him look, as well as sound, like John Bonham.

Aled's song was third in the playing order, by which time the crowd had warmed up a bit. A huge cheer went up when he took over on the drums and immediately launched into 'Rock and Roll', a classic heavy metal Wall of Sound piece requiring huge amounts of driving energy, difficult cymbal work and tricky solo passages. It was a triumph. The Camden Rock Café promoter had been sceptical about Aled's chances. In the event, he was thoroughly impressed. He couldn't

RIGHT
Aled perfects the booming, powerhouse style of heavy metal.

believe that Aled had only been playing for a couple of months. It sounded like he had been playing for years.

John Bonham is now dead and had been an all-round bad boy. Aled isn't like him at all, but he did allow himself a single beer after the show – very rock and roll.

The final challenge

But Aled's musical journey was not yet over. After a chance meeting on his radio show, pop legend Chris de Burgh invited Aled to play the drums with him at a huge gig in Düsseldorf, Germany. Since Chris de Burgh was much more in tune with Aled's musical taste he jumped at the chance.

And so Aled found himself playing live in front of 10,000 German pop fans. The tune was 'Raging Storm', a slow number where the drums do not start until three minutes into the song. It was yet another musical contrast.

Whereas Led Zeppelin's 'Rock and Roll' was all about thundering out a heavy beat – almost violently assaulting the drum kit – the Chris de Burgh song required more finesse and a wider range of techniques – gentle control taps on the cymbals, and subtle little runs on the tom-toms. In similar mellow mood, Aled also played the congas on de Burgh's show-stopper 'Lady in Red'.

Aled had been extremely nervous about appearing in front of such a massive crowd. There was huge potential for embarrassment if he did not get the start of the drum pattern exactly right, since it came in so late in the song. But Aled pulled it off with typical professionalism – even if his teacher Erik Stams (a huge heavy metal fan) said that the tune overall was 'about as exciting as skimmed milk'. 'All in all,' Aled says, 'the process of learning the drums is very rewarding, if you are prepared to put in the effort.'

'There's lots of positives,' he says. 'You feel incredibly empowered. It's a great release of energy and also it makes you appreciate music more. When I listen to music on the radio now, I hear it differently. I used to be interested in the melody and how you would sing it. But now I listen for the drum beat and try to work out how they are doing it – what standard beat or pattern they are using, how they are varying it. It's a totally different approach.'

Chapter 5

Buying an instrument

First instruments

If you are setting out to learn an orchestral instrument like the violin, clarinet or trumpet, it is almost always more sensible to hire an instrument at first to see how you get on with it. Using a reputable hire company or music shop should guarantee you get a useable instrument. The hire company is normally able to carry out any minor repairs and may even be able to give you advice on the type of instrument that would suit you, and when it is time to trade up (see pages 85–9 for ideas of price).

In the first months of playing, the quality of the sound you produce will depend far more on developing technique than the quality of the instrument. A factory-made violin or flute – often from a range aimed at the school-aged learner – is perfectly sufficient. Things are different with guitars and banjos, though, partly because so many types have been developed for different styles of play and types of player. The only remotely 'standard' guitar is the Spanish type, but even with this instrument there is considerable variation in size, tone and playing action.

'An uncle of mine emigrated and couldn't take his guitar with him. When I found it in the attic, I'd found a friend for life.'

STING, SINGER-SONGWRITER AND GUITARIST

When it comes to electrical or rock and roll instruments, the hire market is really aimed at professional musicians, and is based around the supply of amplification and stage gear. It can make sense for professional groups and performers to hire their equipment for each performance or recording session, rather than transport mountains of amplification around from concert to concert, and then store it between times. This, together with the vulnerability of electric guitars to damage and wear and tear at gigs, means that charges for hire and insurance are very steep – around £100 a day. In this market, then, the cost of hiring an instrument is likely to exceed the cost of buying the same instrument within two or three weeks. The same applies to other rock and pop group instruments including drum kits, bass guitars, saxophones and electronic keyboards.

Whatever instrument you are buying, take a teacher or more experienced player with you as there are many pitfalls that the novice might not be aware of. ❚

Buying a guitar

The bottom line with any guitar, for a beginner, is playability. This means it must have an easy playing 'action' – the ease with which the strings can be held against the fret board with the left hand – and it must stay in tune when being played. Here are some things to look out for.

The instrument's tone

Tone in an acoustic guitar is created by the way the body resonates, and the shape, size and condition of the body will all affect the tone. You need to look out for cracks in the body of the instrument, signs of warping and bending on surfaces intended to be flat and, also, for any cracks or stress marks on the joins between the different parts of the body. Any of these problems will adversely affect the tone of the instrument.

The sound of a cheaply bought beginner's electric guitar can be instantly improved by adding better quality pick-ups (a fairly routine if expensive procedure), or by plugging it into a better quality or louder amplifier.

The ability to be tuned

Guitars get out of tune very easily, but one that isn't very well made will be very difficult to tune in the first place. So watch out for a bent or warped neck. If there is movement in these areas, the strings will lift slightly above the fret board, reducing the quality of the playing action, making it difficult to play. Good quality guitars are easier to tune, can hold notes more accurately and stay in tune for longer because they are more 'solid'. They use materials like hardwood for the neck and fret board, which are less likely to warp when the strings are tightened.

> 'Sometimes you want to give up the guitar, you'll hate the guitar. But if you stick with it, you're gonna be rewarded.'
>
> JIMI HENDRIX, GUITARIST

The machine heads

Even if a guitar is solid enough to withstand the pressures of tuning, there may still

Fender TELECASTER

be problems with the tuning pegs, or 'machine heads' as they are sometimes called. The best quality guitars have 'planetary'-type gears, which are easy to turn but, at the same time, are unlikely to slip. At the other extreme, cheaply made guitars have less accurate cog systems. Cheaper machine heads are also more likely to get jammed, to snap or to corrode.

The playing action

If an experienced guitarist praises an instrument for having a good or 'low' action, it means the strings are close to the surface of the fret board, making it easier to press them down, to hold chords and to change quickly from one chord pattern to another. Modern acoustic and all solid body electric guitars have flat bridges, securing the strings just a few millimetres above the flat body, just above the pick-ups (in the case on an electric guitar) and almost flush with the fret board.

The frets should be inset into the fret board and protrude only very slightly. If they stick out too far, the action will be high and it will be difficult to play. If the frets are too low, you will have to place your fingers more accurately in order to get the right note.

The shape of the neck

The shape of the neck varies from guitar to guitar. Generally a thick V-shaped neck is stronger, and therefore less likely to bend or warp, but it is then harder to play. A slim-line neck has a smoother action but, on a cheap guitar, it is likely to bend or warp more quickly. It makes sense, then, to choose a guitar with the thickest neck you feel comfortable with. **I**

Buying a banjo

Banjos produce sound in a similar way to an acoustic guitar, and so many of the same quality considerations apply. However, they are generally far more expensive than beginner guitars, so you are likely to want to keep it for a long time, perhaps for life. Resonator-type banjos have circular wooden rims, and the quality of the wood determines the quality of the sound. Cheaper instruments are made of plywood, better ones of hardwood. In general, the heavier the wood, the greater the tonal range.

A banjo's tone is also affected by its head and tone ring. The head is the white circle made from parchment or plastic that fits over the rim. The thicker the head, the quieter but richer the tone. The tone ring is a circular piece of metal that attaches the head to the rim. If the tone ring is made of a cheap material, such as aluminium, it will have an unattractive, tinny sound.

Buying a piano

A piano is not only a musical instrument, it is also a minor engineering miracle (with up to 10,000 moving parts) and a huge piece of household furniture (probably your largest, and certainly your heaviest and least mobile).

Piano come in two types. The classic form of the instrument is the table-like grand piano, which comes in a variety of sizes from the 'baby' to the 'concert'. You can even buy an electric grand that takes up very little space but has all the attributes of an acoustic grand piano. A concert grand piano may be over three metres in length and 150cm wide. It would occupy an entire living room in an average-sized home, and can simply be too big and heavy to fit into any other sort of domestic space. A 'baby' grand, on the other hand, sits within an area measuring 150 x 150cm. The price of a grand can be prohibitively expensive – the cheapest will set you back several thousand pounds, but you might be able to get a re-conditioned second-hand instrument for as little as £1,000.

Upright pianos, however, are usually less expensive than grand pianos, although top of the range uprights are every bit as expensive as a small grand piano. They can also be accommodated more easily.

No instrument is quite so dependent on the quality of manufacture as the piano, at least in the beginner and intermediate league, so take care in choosing one. Unlike antique furniture and hand-crafted quality violins, pianos do not tend to improve with age, as many people might believe. The instrument does not age well because of the tremendous stresses the piano wires exert on the internal metal frame. The frame will tend to warp over time, especially if it is kept in less than ideal conditions. After that it will be very difficult to tune.

Buying an electronic keyboard

On cheaper instruments, the keys are not 'touch sensitive', meaning that they will play a note at the same loudness, however hard the key is pressed. These instruments are best avoided as are keyboards with scaled-down keys. Also choose a keyboard with at least 60 piano-sized keys (a traditional piano has 88 keys), which is perfectly adequate as an educational tool.

A brand new, good-quality factory-built piano would be expected to stay in excellent condition – good enough for professional performance or recording – for 20 years. With luck, good maintenance and tender loving care it might last as long again. After that, a piano will almost certainly begin to show its age. A 50-year-old piano is unlikely to pay its way on the professional music circuit, but it could well be good enough – and affordable enough – for good quality amateur work, and certainly good enough for a beginner to practise on.

If you are looking to buy a second-hand piano, take someone who knows about pianos with you. Professional piano tuners will look over a piano for about the same cost as a tuning session and provide an opinion. Make sure that the mid range of keys are working properly and are in tune. The very high and very low notes tend to 'go' first in older pianos, but this needn't be a drawback for the beginner (or even an experience amateur player) because the extreme notes are rarely used. Check, too, that you like the 'feel' of the keys (how much pressure you need to apply and if you can play softly and loudly) and the piano's tone.

Whatever else you do, make sure you that you don't end up with a real wreck, where the metal frame is so badly warped (or even cracked) that the instrument cannot be accurately tuned. You do see such ancient instruments in church halls and used essentially as heritage-style furniture pieces in houses, pubs and hotels. But it is unlikely that they could ever again be tuned to concert pitch.

Looking after your piano

Whether you have an upright or grand piano, it needs tuning about twice a year. The instrument also needs to be kept in environmentally perfect conditions, so try not to position your piano right next to a radiator or in a damp room as the case and frame can become warped. ▌

Insurance

Insuring musical instruments can be an expensive business, too. Specialist insurance companies do exist, such as Allianz Cornhill Musical Insurance at www.allianzcornhillmusicalinsurance.co.uk. You can also add your instrument as a named high value, or high risk, item on your household contents insurance. There is a big difference in premiums if you want to cover potential loss of an instrument from your car. The following examples cover loss, theft or damage of the instrument anywhere in the UK and Europe, including theft from a car.

Electric guitar worth £200	**Premium: £30 per year**
Saxophone worth £500	**Premium: £32 per year**
Violin worth £4,500	**Premium: £42 per year**

Buying a string instrument

The violin is the most common orchestral instrument. It also has a role in folk, country and – to a much lesser extent – rock and pop music. It is therefore a very popular instrument and so student level instruments are plentiful in the shops – and you can't really go wrong with the ubiquitous Stentor range of beginner violins. Such mass-produced, factory-fresh instruments are relatively cheap to buy and you can hire them, too (see page 86). The same applies to violas and cellos.

The second-hand market for string instruments is complicated and needs to be approached with extreme caution. Everyone has heard of the huge value of old master violins, such as Stradivarius (he made violas and cellos, too), and many assume that all string instruments improve in quality and become more valuable with age. This is far from always being the case. The tone of modern factory-made instruments will improve with playing, but they are not going to improve in value because they are made with relatively cheap materials to begin with.

> 'When buying a bow, think of spending about 25 per cent of the value of the instrument.'
>
> CASWELLS, INSTRUMENT DEALERS

Buying or trading in second-hand string instruments is a difficult and hazardous business and should be left to experts. But if you are buying an instrument – new or second hand – there are a few simple quality indicators you need to look out for.

Tuning pegs

The first is the condition of the four tuning pegs that are used to tighten the strings. These should not be splintered and should fit securely into the corresponding holes in the scroll. The pegs are used to tune the instrument and to produce most of the tension on the strings. In addition, many violins have fine tuning screws with adjustable levers, behind the bridge. Make sure these are not corroded and jammed and that, in general, they are easy to use. Unless the tuning mechanisms are in tip-top condition, the instrument will be very hard to tune, and may not stay in tune very well either.

edc

The fingerboard

In second-hand instruments, check that the fingerboard is not too worn. Constant playing produces depressions along the fingerboard at points where the fingers hold down the strings. These distortions can make the instrument hard to play even if it is otherwise a good-quality antique with excellent tone produced by its ancient wood. Refurbishment of a worn fingerboard is a difficult and expensive process and may, in fact, be impossible without destroying the balance of the instrument and its overall tone.

The sound post

A problem with any string instrument, new or old, is for the sound post – an internal, pencil-thin wooden rod that holds apart the top and bottom curved panels of the body – to snap or come loose. If this happens, the instrument will lose all its tone and there is the possibility of the belly cracking. It is possible for a broken or loose sound post to be repaired using special instruments.

Cracks and warps

More obviously, be very wary of any sort of cracks in the body. Small cracks can be repaired, but the instrument's tone may have been spoilt. There is a danger, too, that the neck may warp or be pulled into an untenable bent shape by the tension of the strings. You can check this hasn't happened by looking for signs of stress, breakage or repairs at the point where the neck joins the body. In the same way, the instrument should have an easy and responsive playing action, meaning that the strings are stretched clear above the fingerboard, but not so far that they are hard to hold down. ▌

Buying a bow

A bow is just as important as the instrument itself, and varies in weight and length depending on whether it's for a violin, viola or cello. If you are buying a new instrument, a bow and case are often included in the 'kit', but they can be bought separately as well. You can buy bows second hand, but beware hairs falling out or a warped bow. If you are buying a cheaper instrument second hand, it is probably worth investing in a new bow, because it will work out cheaper than getting the existing one re-haired or suffering from a poorly balanced bow if it is warped. Cheap bows can be bought for under £20 each. For something a little better made, think of spending around £100; if it's top-notch quality you are after, you could easily move into four figures.

A block of rosin, to keep the bow sticky, is needed. A £5 block of rosin should last many years.

Buying a woodwind instrument

As a beginner, it will almost certainly be better to hire rather than buy a woodwind instrument. For the cost of buying and hiring, see page 89.

Buying a clarinet

Clarinets do not age well. The instrument has to be taken to bits to be cleaned and packed away and, eventually, the airtight seals between the sections loosen and leak. When that happens, it is difficult to keep the instrument in tune, so before buying, ensure the seals are tight. In addition, make sure that none of the keys are jammed and air can't escape from the instrument through any cracks or gaps.

Buying a saxophone

A 'good' saxophone will have leather padding on the keys rather than cork or rubber. The cheaper materials will do the job of making the instrument airtight, but will not age as well. Corrosion can be a problem and more expensive instruments use stainless steel springs to prevent sticking. Check the keys aren't jammed, the padding hasn't perished and there are no cracks.

Buying a flute

The crucial quality factor for a flute is the solidity and quality of the 'nickel-silver' alloy (a mixture of copper, zinc and nickel) used to produce most instruments. More expensive instruments are plated with real silver or an additional layer of pure nickel. Plating delays corrosion and makes the action of the keys smoother. A thick layer of silver plating also improves the tone of the instrument.

Check there are no bends or dents along the length of the instrument. You also need to look at the type of blowhole and lip plate employed. Better makes have slightly curved lip plates, making it easier for the lips to seal the blowhole.

Also check that all moving parts are working correctly. The pads that seal the keys should lie flat over the holes with no gap and the springs should be working properly, returning the keys firmly, smoothly and noiselessly to the open position when they aren't being depressed. Ideally, the springs should be made from stainless steel. Be very wary of any sign of rust or corrosion around the springs. ▌

Buying a brass instrument

When buying a brass instrument, you need to concentrate on the mouthpiece. The rest of the body is less critical to begin with, although the valves do need to move easily and freely. There are many types of mouthpiece, and the most advanced players customise their own to some extent. Most teachers would recommend that you start with a simple, curved 'C-cup'-type mouthpiece, which is the standard mouthpiece found on most makes of student-level instruments. It is possible that a second-hand trumpet previously used by an advanced player may have been fitted with a custom-shaped mouthpiece, which is more difficult to play, so remember to check this point.

Buying a trumpet

Buying second hand is an option with trumpets because there aren't many moving parts. The valve mechanism is relatively simple (compared with that of, say, a piano) and so there is less to go wrong. As with all metallic instruments, the main problems to look out for in older ones are corrosion and worn areas, especially around moving parts.

Corrosion inside the instrument is very hard to spot, except indirectly by getting an experienced player to demonstrate a few scales. Internal rot makes it very hard to reproduce or hold notes accurately. In the worst cases, internal corrosion can be detected as small, pinkish-brown spots or blotches on the brass exterior. If you see this, the internal corrosion is so bad that it is about to eat a hole clean through to the exterior of the instrument. Dents, scuffs and scratches are less of a problem and may even add to the charm and character of an instrument (though vastly reduce resale value).

> 'The thicker the brass, the heavier the instrument and therefore the darker the sound.'
>
> CHAPPELL, INSTRUMENT STORE

Buying a drum kit

There is huge wear and tear on stick-beaten drums and cymbals and the main problem with cheaper drum kits is that they will fall apart more quickly (see page 89 for ideas of price). However, if you progress with the drums, it very easy to replace the original, relatively cheap component drums with better makes, and with additional drums and cymbals. Drummers in the rock supergroups of the Seventies and Eighties would sometimes appear behind dozens of cymbals and huge arrays of tom-tom drums arranged by size. Kits like these gave drummers a wider range of tonal possibilities. Fashions have changed and, these days, rock drum kits are smaller, producing rhythmically simpler and crisper bass drum, snare and hi-hat patterns.

If you buy (or add) second-hand drums to your kit, check that they are in the correct circular shape without warping. The drum skins, top and bottom, can be replaced fairly cheaply if they are worn, but if the locking mechanism and tuning lugs that stretch the skins are jammed or too loose, then the cost of refurbishment is likely to be prohibitive.

> 'Check out the robustness of the fittings and mounts; they are frequently a source of trouble on cheaper kits.'
>
> DRUMWRIGHT, SPECIALIST DRUM STORE

Because of the problems of finding a practice place, many drummers – beginners and the more experienced alike – need to buy a set of near-silent practice pads. Pads allow you to learn how to play the drums without driving your neighbours insane. There are two types – pads that lie like rubber mats over the actual drums, deadening the sound; and complete 'kits' consisting of non-resonating silent wooden or rubber blocks.

'There's no frustration,
really. Whatever you
do sounds beautiful.'

Diane Abbott plays the piano

LEFT
For Diane, practice was never a chore. A little effort produced a lot of progress.

In 1987, Diane Abbott made history by becoming the first black woman to be elected to the House of Commons. She has served in parliament ever since, as Labour MP for the inner city London constituency of Hackney, where she now lives.

Diane was born in Paddington in 1953, two years after her parents arrived in London from Jamaica. Her family was relatively poor and were not especially interested in music. They listened to a mixture of mainstream pop and West Indian music, but had no spare money to pay for music lessons, even if Diane had wanted them, which she didn't. Until very recently, music played only a small role in her life.

'At school there might have been music going on,' she says, 'but it passed me by. If I thought about it, it did seem like a thing posh middle class kids did, and that wasn't me. It wasn't something I felt excluded from, though lessons would have been a luxury our family wouldn't really have been able to afford if I had wanted them. Playing music was just something that didn't crop up. It was something that other people did.'

In her teens, Diane was anyway working hard and doing well at school. Eventually she won a place at Cambridge University, where she read history. 'As a teenager obviously I listened to pop music like everyone else, but anything more than that – I didn't have an interest. My passion was books, and later politics. I was a text person – that and the visual arts. I continued to enjoy music, but it was in the background. I just about knew what I liked, but beyond that music was a closed book.'

At Cambridge, Diane threw herself into the 'world of ideas and argument', as she puts it. Looking back, especially in the light of her recently developed interest in music, she regrets that she did not get involved in the music scene at university: 'At Cambridge there was a lot of classical music – recitals, all types of events and lots of musicians and people who knew about music. I didn't take much advantage of that, and now I wish I had.'

After Cambridge, Diane worked for the National Council for Civil Liberties (the civil rights organisation now called Liberty) and at the Greater London Council as a media relations officer. In a time of much more polarised politics, Diane was at or near the centre of huge and bitter controversies and clashes between left and right in politics. There was little time for music, or anything else, in those heady days. Worse than that, there might have been some people on the political left who regarded classical music as irredeemably bourgeois.

'I come from a working class family,' Diane says. 'And I don't accept that classical music is bourgeois. My family in Jamaica were involved in music and they were poor farmers.'

It was one relative in particular that caught Diane's imagination, her Uncle Adrian. West Indian culture is, of course, famous for some of the world's most dynamic and captivating forms of folk and pop music – from calypso and blues to reggae and jazz. There is also a heritage of church music, popularised as gospel and soul music.

But Diane's Uncle Adrian was not a folk or soul singer, nor a church organist. He was a talented and highly proficient classical violinist. This is less surprising than it might at first seem. In some ways, rural Jamaica keeps alive a genteel and charmingly old-fashioned version of English civility and good manners. Respect for classical piano playing – an important badge of middle class respectability, especially for girls – is part of all that.

Diane never met her Uncle Adrian. He was more of a family legend. But the moving story of his achievements against the odds – and his failure to reach this full potential because of segregation and racism – is what inspired Diane to learn to play classical piano.

'I was always intrigued by my Uncle Adrian,' Diane says. 'He was a poor farmer from a small farm in Jamaica. How did he manage to learn the violin?' It turned out that he had moved for a while to New York where, in the 1920s, he managed to take lessons with the famous black classical violinist Felix Weir and may have, for a time, been associated with the world reknowned Julliard School of Music.

'Because he was black,' she explains, 'he was not allowed to register formally for lessons. This was depression era America, and there was racism and strict segregation. He went along to learn, but had to sit at the back. If he went to any of the music schools or to Carnegie Hall, he had to go in by the back door.'

In 1929, Uncle Adrian arrived back in Jamaica. 'He used to give recitals to the Governor of Jamaica and to rich white people,' Diane says. 'But he had to combine playing the violin with earning a living.'

Diane learnt from her uncle's son how sometimes there would be no food in the house. But when Adrian played it did not seem quite so bad. 'My uncle had this passion for the violin,' Diane says, adding: 'He never stopped playing, but he never reached his full potential. He worked with his hands as a farmer and labourer – that's hard work. I do wonder how well he could have done if he had access to proper musical education, time and a little bit of money to practise.

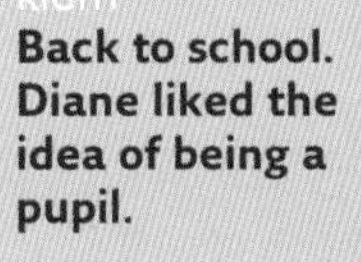

RIGHT
Back to school. Diane liked the idea of being a pupil.

'His son told me that he had so admired his dad that he thought of copying him and taking up the violin as well,' Diane explains. 'But Uncle Adrian warned him off. He didn't want him to try to learn music because he thought he would never be in a position to have lessons or reach his potential. The violin had been very cruel to Uncle Adrian. His passion for the violin had meant he and his family had to struggle.' His son grew up to be a doctor instead.

One positive legacy of Adrian's musical gift was the love of classical music he inspired in members of Diane's family in Jamaica. During a trip to Jamaica she found that Adrian's collection of classical records was still intact and that another uncle, Len, had developed a deep love for the romantic classical piano music of Frederick Chopin.

Diane's musical journey

Diane resolved to honour the memory of her uncle by learning to play at least one Chopin piece on the piano. It was an emotional commitment and a difficult one. She was fantastically busy with a new parliamentary session about to start and she had set herself the deadline of learning to play a prelude by Chopin from scratch in just a few months. There were times when she thought she might not make it.

Diane took to the piano with enthusiasm. 'It's good in your middle years, I think, to do something completely new, and completely different. The worst thing about passing 50 is that you can get stuck in a rut – doing the things you've always done, going back over them. For me, learning the piano is an escape to a different world. I've been in a world of words, or debates, ideas and arguments. But this is all about harmony and emotions. It's so refreshing. Music is something completely different.'

RIGHT
One step at a time. It is best to play scales slowly at first.

There's another thing Diane likes about the process – following instructions rather than being expected to lead, and allowing others to take the decisions for once: 'I love the idea of being a pupil again, and being told what to do. I really enjoy that. And it has opened a whole new world for me.

'The thing that's struck me is the way you get in touch with your emotions. It changes your state of mind and you can blot out all your worries. Chopin's music is very

'It's so refreshing.
Music is something
completely different.'

emotional. In a way it is curiously liberating, because when you are trying to play, it makes you switch off from everything else. You just try and make beautiful sounds. And, to my surprise, a lot of the sounds you make are quite beautiful – even before you learn to play a complete piece.'

Diane found the process enjoyable, but she had to put in a lot of effort. The key for her was taking a relaxed attitude. She set herself the slightly nerve-inducing challenge of performing in public, but she tried not to focus on that. 'I didn't set out thinking I was going to turn into the world's greatest pianist. So the pressure is not there. I couldn't play anything at all before I started. So anything I learn is a bonus. I set out to do this because I wanted to experience a process of learning, not because I wanted to be seen as a great musical genius.'

Diane found that she could 'plod along' making decent progress so long as she practised. She also had the highly experienced Paul Roberts (professor of piano at the Guildhall School of Music & Drama in London) as her teacher and – importantly – established a good working relationship with him. Initially, her main difficulty was the very common one

RIGHT
Diane could play tunes with one hand immediately. Using both hands took a little more time and confidence.

of getting both her hands playing at the same time. She found she could play the notes with the right hand and, with a little more difficulty, she could do the same for the left. But she could not do both at the same time.

To keep her morale up, Diane persuaded established players to play the left-hand part, while she played the right-hand part with one hand. Soon she overcame the problem and, slowly at first, found that she could bring both hands into play – with much more satisfying results.

The final challenge

The challenge Diane took on was the daunting one of performing the Chopin prelude at a recital at St Martin-in-the-Fields in London. She was extremely nervous, even though she had practised the piece over and over and, in the privacy of her own home, could play it perfectly.

Performing in front of a classical audience was another matter, though. After a couple of minutes, she stumbled, had to re-start and – finally – her teacher, Paul Roberts, helped her by playing the left-hand part of the piece. The audience was sympathetic, giving her a rousing round of applause. To go from a standing start to a live performance of a piece of the standard of Chopin's prelude in a few months was a huge achievement. Diane was mildly disappointed, but – determined as ever – vowed to continue her musical journey.

'I didn't realise at first just how difficult that was going to be. When you listen to a recording it sounds very simple. But that's why it's so good. It sounds simple, but it's actually very complex. The challenge is really about getting your hands to move independently from one another.

'I've never been particularly well co-ordinated, so I've had to really practise that, and go at it slowly, systematically. I'm right-handed and I found it difficult to get the left hand going at first, and then getting both hands working together.

'But what I've found is that none of this is really a chore. Once you are away from the performance aspect, there's no frustration with it at all, because whatever you do tends to sound good. You realise with a bit of effort you can play something really very beautiful and that's an incentive. That's enough to keep you going.'

Chapter 6

Performing with your instrument

Joining a jazz or rock group

The pleasure to be had from music is almost always enhanced by playing with others. While there may be new types of difficulty and frustration, it is an excellent way to make friends and playing in a group can also provide motivation and clear goals for practice. Indeed, for many instruments, much of the pleasure and point of playing depends on being able to play with others.

For any drummers out there, you can find drum-only ensembles, normally using hand drums, by searching the Drum Jam Network website at www.drumjam.co.uk/. If you are interested in joining a West African drum group, contact African Drumbeat at www.african-drumbeat.co.uk/. Alternatively, the steel band movement is famously welcoming and the nature of the instrument and the size of the orchestra means there are roles for performers at all levels of ability. For details of your local band, contact the British Association of Steel Bands at www.panonthenet.com/articles/uk/2006/bas-board.htm.

If jazz is your thing, you can find a list of jazz clubs at the excellent Jazz Clubs Worldwide site at www.jazz-clubs-worldwide.com, where you can navigate through comprehensive listings for all jazz clubs and other events. The site also contains contact details for jazz groups looking for particular instrumentalists (and in all styles and at all levels of playing).

To sing a solo or self-accompanied is mainly a matter of turning up at 'open mike' nights in clubs or pubs, where these are advertised in the local press or in 'what's on'-type entertainment guides on the internet. Rock, soul, pop and indie players are less likely to get a 'gig' by turning up at an open mike session, but to balance that there are huge numbers of websites dedicated to forming groups, performing, recording and even publishing music. One of the best sites is Forming Bands at www.formingbands.co.uk.

Opportunities to play as a group will be confined, at least at first, to occasional bookings in pubs and clubs that still provide live music. Booking at smaller places can be arranged informally, but usually the group will have to provide good quality recordings of their music. The first 'gig' is often the most difficult to obtain. The best advice is to accept any offer to perform and use that as a credential to play at steadily larger events and venues.

Schecter

Playing folk music

Folk performance is split between the world of folk-rock playing, which is really an offshoot of pop music, and the serious (sometimes semi-academic) world of traditional folk song and dance.

If you are interested in the former, and in accompanying yourself, or perhaps playing along with one or two others, you can find partners using an internet-based search service such as Forming Bands (see page 206). Group practice on acoustic instruments is less of a daunting problem than for rock bands and can usually be done in the homes of band members, so long as the people they live with are tolerant enough.

Obtaining a gig will then be a matter of finding a singers' night at a pub or club. There's no national federation for this type of performance, other than the Musician's Union. But a simple Google search on the internet should provide a list of open mike nights in your region.

Traditional folk music is often associated with the dance forms it is used to accompany, such as Morris dancing in England and other forms of traditional ceilidh dancing. You can explore the world of traditional and 'cross-over' or 'fusion' folk music using the *Direct Roots* directory (available from bookshops or from www.folkarts-england.org). There you will find associations specialising in different national and regional folk traditions, and, in particular, instruments and styles of playing (for example, Irish fiddle playing or American bluegrass banjo). These associations tend to organise their own gatherings, lessons, festivals and performances.

> 'There's one moment every year when the crowd sings and the band stops playing. It doesn't get any better than that really.'
>
> SIMON NICOL, GUITARIST AND VOCALIST, FAIRPORT CONVENTION

The British Banjo, Mandolin and Guitar Federation at www.banjomandolinguitar.co.uk/ lists folk guitar and banjo festivals, the activities of groups of local enthusiasts and other performance opportunities.

Playing in a brass band or orchestra

Unless you plan to play in a classical orchestra or a steel band, the best way to experience the huge thrill of playing in a very large group is to join a brass band. The British brass band movement was once based around either nonconformist churches and chapels (as an alternative to the more High Church tradition of pipe organ playing) and coal mining and factory communities, mainly in Wales and the North of England. You can find details for your local brass band by contacting the British Federation of Brass Bands at www.bfbb.co.uk.

Cities and towns across the UK boast amateur symphony orchestras and a range of chamber ensembles, sometimes connected with larger churches, local authority adult education department and charitable trusts. Most of these groups will expect players to have reached grade eight, or something like it, in their mastery of their instrument.

> 'It's a fantastic moment when you realise it's a fellowship and you meet other people who have respect and reverence for this music.'
>
> ERIC CLAPTON, GUITARIST

The amateur musical life of the UK is vibrant and your teacher – if you have taken on a classical instrument – will certainly know of an amateur orchestra or appropriate local chamber group. In addition, there is an excellent national web-based clearing house at www.amateurorchestras.org.uk. The site is organised by region and in London, for example, lists almost 100 classical music groups, including many orchestras. In each case, the site gives contact details and an idea of the level of playing that is expected or required.

'It's an underdog instrument. But there's just something about it. Even the name makes you smile.'

Frank Skinner plays the banjo

Frank Skinner fast became a household name in the 1990s, winning the Perrier Award in 1991, breaking ratings records with his co-star David Baddiel in BBC1's *Fantasy Football League*, and then attracting over 7 million viewers per episode as the star of his own BBC1 chat show, *The Frank Skinner Show*. In 1997, he ended his 100-date national stand-up tour at a specially constructed Battersea Power Station in front of 6,500 people. The gig itself got into the *Guinness Book of Records* as Britain's largest ever solo comedy performance.

Together with his comedy partner, David Baddiel, and the band The Lightning Seeds, Frank also wrote 'Three Lions' ('It's Coming Home'), the most popular football anthem ever. The record went to Number One in the charts, first in 1996, as the England Euro '96 single, and then for a second time in 1998, as the official England World Cup theme. Frank described the experience of seeing the massed ranks of England fans singing 'Three Lions' at Wembley as 'the best moment of my life.' In 2002, Frank published his bestselling autobiography. In 2006, he covered the World Cup in Germany in a series of chart-topping podcasts for *The Times*. When Frank took on the *Play it Again* challenge he was half-way through writing his first novel. He thought that the practical and hopefully absorbing process of learning to play a musical instrument would provide some balance to his life.

Frank Skinner was born in 1957 under the name Chris Collins and grew up in the Birmingham suburb of Oldbury. The name change resulted when, at the start of his stage career, Frank found out that the name 'Chris Collins' had already been registered by another performer. He named himself after a member of his dad's pub dominos team instead.

LEFT
Frank gets twangy with his prized bluegrass banjo.

Growing up in the 1960s, Frank was influenced by his older brother, who collected Fifties rock and roll records and filled the house with the sound of Elvis Presley and Jerry Lee Lewis. 'Everyone else was getting into pop,' Frank remembers, 'but my brother was playing rock and roll in the house. So I was a decade behind everyone else.'

Although always seen as an intelligent lad, as a teenager Frank's prospects did not seem good. He did not do well at school and eventually went to work in a local foundry, but hated the work. 'We hammered lumps of metal into shape,' he says in his autobiography. 'Everyone there was deaf and had three fingers.' At the same time Frank was drinking heavily. He formed a heavy metal group called Olde English with some mates – but they threw him out because, they later cheerfully claimed, Frank was always drinking, turning up late and missing band practice.

In the mid-1980s Frank was at a low point in his life. He turned it around by going to night school and by studying for a degree in English literature at what was then Birmingham Polytechnic. 'Johnny Cash made me an alcoholic,' Frank has said, 'but English literature saved my life.' At that time he took a vow that, whatever else he was doing, he would always make sure he was on a course of some sort, learning a new skill or developing a new interest.

In 1986, Frank began his a career as a stand-up comedian, putting his experience of the rough side of life together with a natural, biting, quick wit to work on the stage. He also rode the rising tide of interest in football. Frank is a fanatical supporter of 'The Baggies' (West Bromwich Albion FC) and, unlike the newly fashionable enthusiasm for the televised game expressed by many performers and politicians in the Nineties – Frank is the real thing – a lifelong fan with an understanding of the importance of the game in working class life. At the same time, he gave up drinking for good. He now describes himself as a recovering alcoholic.

Frank's musical journey

When Frank took on the *Play it Again* challenge, he chose the banjo, largely because it is such a minority instrument and, as he says, just about the most 'uncool' instrument in the world. 'I went into a big music store in London,' he says, 'and there were shelves and shelves full of tutors and books about playing the guitar. There in the corner were about eight books about the banjo. I was pleased that I was getting involved with something so unpopular.' At the same time, Frank found something intrinsically joyful about the instrument. 'It makes this sort of explosion of sound,' he says. 'It is the ultimate folk instrument. All other instruments, including the guitar, have a classical equivalent, but I don't think there's an orchestra anywhere in the world with a banjo. It's an underdog instrument. But there's just something about it that cheers you up ... even the name makes you smile.'

Frank could already play the guitar, but only enough to accompany himself by strumming chords. This meant that the process of forming chord shapes with his left hand was familiar, but the banjo is tuned and strung in a completely different way, and so a whole new set of chord shapes would have to be learnt. At the same time, while Frank was used to strumming guitar strings, he would have to master various styles of 'finger-picking'. On the banjo, each string has to be plucked individually with the thumb and each finger of the

RIGHT
Frank doing some nervous practice at the international banjo contest.

right hand. He would also have to learn to play with a set of metal picks on the fingers of his right hand.

Frank set off at a furious pace, breaking off from writing his novel to practise for at least two hours a day. He also kept a 'video diary' of his practice sessions for his teacher Pete Stanley, a veteran banjo player and star of the folk circuit, so that he could further his playing skills. Delighted by his successes, Frank started telling people that he had 'fallen in love' with the banjo and wanted to play it more and more. He loved the shape of it, the way he could just pick it up and improvise on it ... everything about it was just great.

RIGHT
It's not as easy as it looks, but with patience and practice, Frank began to fall in love with his banjo.

Going public

Frank's first public performance on the banjo came just about a month after he had met Pete for the first time. He was able to join a band of Birmingham banjo enthusiasts playing in an old folk's home. Despite the fact that Frank sometimes lost his way during the performance, he enjoyed the performance. Things could only get better.

As part of the *Play it Again* challenge, Frank was due to compete in an international banjo competition in Kansas, the home of bluegrass music, which required that he learnt to play with all five fingers. Some banjo players would take 10 years or more before they perfected the all-important five-digit 'rolls'. Frank had just 10 weeks.

After a couple of weeks covering the World Cup in Germany for *The Times*, Frank experienced a 'banjo crisis'. During his time away, he'd played the banjo now and again and had tried to keep his practice going, but he had naturally slackened off from his rigorous practising, and now found he had forgotten how to pick some tunes that he previously thought he had got under his fingers. He felt he was going backwards, and was suddenly seized with self-doubt. It had happened to him before: 'In the past I've tried to learn all sorts of things – horse riding, ice skating, salsa dancing, the tango, French. It's always the same pattern. Starts off well and I think, "Oh, I'm doing really well here; maybe I'm a natural." And then – thump! – I hit a wall and I can't do it.'

In order to get back on track, Frank changed his teacher, taking lessons instead from John Dowling,

‘It makes this joyful explosion of sound. It’s the ultimate folk instrument.’

Frank Skinner plays the banjo

a British-based champion of the Kansas banjo competition he was going to enter. 'I need to progress in a series of concrete steps,' Frank said of his first teacher. 'Pete is obsessed with the banjo and, like a lot of people who are really good at something, he sometimes forgets – or can't imagine – that other people aren't as good as him. It was great to have lessons from him right at the start. He inspired me. But he's a free spirit. He loves performing and it's natural to him. But I needed more of a structure.'

To Frank's relief, in addition to demonstrating virtuosity, John took a more systematic approach to teaching the banjo, emphasising drills and warm-up exercises. After two weeks of intensive lessons and practice, Frank once again felt confident. He was now playing the piece he would perform at the competition – 'John Hardy' – with all his fingers, just like a proper banjo player. It was slow at first, but with practice, came growing fluency.

The final challenge

Frank arrived at the Winfield Bluegrass Festival and began to mingle with the 20,000 other people there, feeling

RIGHT
Frank was never going to win the Kansas banjo championship, but he was warmly welcomed, made friends and had a great time.

alternately confident and nervous. On the eve of the contest, though, Frank joined one of the knots of bluegrass players busking simple tunes. To his great delight, he found that he felt at home in the company of players at all levels and that he could fit right in.

The combination of meeting such skilled players and the huge commitment they had to the banjo, made Frank look at the instrument in a whole new way. He found the social side of banjo playing fascinating. Of course, the best players were insanely competitive, but at the same time, everyone was welcome, whatever their level. At least, until the competition got under way.

Fortunately for Frank, he had already decided that he was not going to be competing at the highest level anyway. As a result, he was reasonably relaxed, seeing entry into the contest as a stepping-stone in his own learning process. So he stepped up and played 'John Hardy'. There were mistakes, but he managed to play the whole piece right through without actually coming to a halt. The crowd was mildly impatient, but kind about his performance and they gave him a warm, if muted, round of applause for being so game.

'I was bad – I was really bad,' Frank said the moment he came off stage. 'I got nervous – it started to go wrong, and once it started to go wrong, it got worse and worse. It really was the worst I've played it for a long time.' Later on, Frank reflected that, although he had pretty much ploughed it in the competition, he had gained a huge amount from the experience. For a start, he could stop practising 'John Hardy' and find a tune that was much closer to his level. After mastering that, he could then move on tune-by-tune, learning by ear and using tabs just as Pete had intended.

'I didn't understand the bluegrass thing before I did this,' Frank ruminated. 'The highlight for me was playing "Somebody Robbed The Glendale Train" in the moonlight with a bunch of people I had never met before in my life. It was a fantastic experience ... I was honoured to be among people who were just that good at something I want to be good at. They were inspirational. It is not about competitions. It's about being able to sit out there – even with complete strangers – and join in a kind of universal language.'

Directory of information

Why play music?

- Dr Norman Weinberger of the University of California's work on music and wellbeing: www.musica.uci.edu/index.html
- Music, mental health and brain function; notes from the Massachusetts Institute of Technology Media lab: www.media.mit.edu/hyperins/projects/music_mind_health.html
- Research into the effect of music on depression: www.enterthefreudianslip.com/music_therapy_and_depression.htm
- Controlled breathing: www.petethomas.co.uk/saxophone-diaphragm.html
- Indiana University on 'The Mozart Effect': www.indiana.edu/~intell/mozarteffect2.shtml
- New Horizons Band in the US aimed at people taking up instruments later in life; at present US based but there are plans to spread across the world: www.newhorizonsmusic.org/nhima.htm
- Cool Edit Pro: professional standard digital recording, editing and mixing software; record your own multi-track music. Free trial: www.softpedia.com/progDownload/Cool-Edit-Pro-Download-2076.html

Are you musical?

- Free online hearing test: www.freehearingtest.com/test.shtml
- University of New South Wales, online test of relative 'tone deafness' or 'perfect pitch': www.phys.unsw.edu.au/~jw/hearing.html
- US National Institute on Deafness and Other Communication Disorders; free online test of relative 'tone deafness': www.nidcd.nih.gov/tunetest/

Which instrument?

Below are some sites that give a general introduction to various types of music, or to an instrument or group of instruments. Explore these links if you are looking for inspiration or not yet sure about your musical direction.

Rock, pop and reggae

- Rock Revolution: comprehensive guide to the history and scope of music that represented a social revolution: http://library.advanced.org/18249/
- Outer Sound: the world of 'indie' and alternative guitar-based rock music: www.outersound.com/
- Jammin' Reggae Archives: for reggae players and enthusiasts: http://niceup.com/

Jazz and blues

- All About Jazz: international magazine and directory of jazz websites, based in the USA: www.allaboutjazz.com/
- Redhouse Jazz: encouraging women to play jazz and jazz instruments: http://home.comcast.net/~stotko/red/
- Blues World: directory of hundreds of sites devoted to guitar-based blues music: www.bluesworld.com/index.html

Folk, country and bluegrass

- British and traditional American folk music: www.contemplator.com/folk.html
- The English Folk Dance and Song Society: www.efdss.org
- Traditional and 'cross-over' or 'fusion' folk music using the Direct Roots directory: www.folkarts-england.org
- Nashville Network: clearing house for country music sites – history, playing technique, profiles of stars: www.givemenashville.com/Nashville_Music_Page.htm
- Specialist American bluegrass/country banjo playing site; discussion groups, online advice, notification of events: www.bluegrassworld.com

Classical

- Symphonic music: LSO Discovery, a free introductory educational programme run by the London Symphony Orchestra designed for people who want to start to play or appreciate classical music: www.lso.co.uk/lsodiscovery/
- Contemporary classical music: an archive featuring the music from the world of contemporary music: www.arcmusic.org/begin.html

Community and religious performance

- The Brass Band Webring: www.harrogate.co.uk/harrogate-band/webring.htm
- British Federation of Brass Bands: www.bfbb.co.uk
- Steel band music: www.pan-jumbie.com/linksUK.htm
- Church music, including organ playing: www.churchmusic.org.uk/urlsearch.php/related
- Jewish music: www.jmi.org.uk/
- Sufi Islamic music: www.sufimusic.org/

World music

- World music on the BBC: www.bbc.co.uk/radio3/worldmusic/index.shtml
- WOMAD: World Music Arts and Dance: http://womad.org/

Getting started

- Learn to read music with online multimedia lessons: www.musictheory.net/
- Music education software for a large variety of instruments,

and for learning music theory: http://musicked.com/

- Computer-assisted music making Garage Band: Apple Corp's combined composition and performance tool; expensive software, but there's a free tour here: www.apple.com/ilife/garageband/
- 'Voice-to-Note' software: sing into a microphone and the computer transcribes the sound into music, and then plays the tune using the sound of an instrument such as the piano; costs about £20: www.musicmasterworks.com/index.htm
- Educational Software Co-operative (music department): large range of music education 'shareware' – everything from transcription of classical music for guitar picking, to automated hearing tests, music theory lessons and simple composition aids: www.edu-soft.org/padlib/
- Notepad: free music composition software: www.finalemusic.com/notepad/

Guitar

- Online guitar tuning: www.8notes.com/guitar_tuner
- Ultimate Guitar: huge site with hundreds of simple guitar chord and solo tabs for well-known rock and pop tunes: www.ultimate-guitar.com
- E-chords: online video guitar lessons, shows you how to form chords; huge online library of chord shapes: www.e-chords.com
- Website for buying strings: www.stringmail.co.uk

Piano

- The Piano House: automated online tutor demonstrating how to play chords and scales. Shows each key in the chord being depressed and plays the corresponding tone: www.looknohands.com/chordhouse/piano
- Free online library of midi tunes, demonstrating common practice pieces: www.classicalmidiconnection.com/cmc/handel.html

Other instruments

Online advice, lessons, free sheet music and directories of teachers:

- Clarinet: www.musicalresources.co.uk/clarinet.php
- Saxophone: www.saxontheweb.net/Links.html
- Flute: www.8notes.com/flute/
- Violin: www.violinandviola.co.uk/
- Trumpet: www.8notes.com/trumpet/
- Drums: www.drum-tech.co.uk/

Formal education and grade exams

- Associated Board of the Royal Schools of Music (ABRSM); music grade exams in all major instruments – classical and jazz styles: www.abrsm.org
- Trinity Guildhall College; wide range of formal musical education, including grade exams: www.trinitycollege.co.uk

Buying an instrument

- Guitar: www.ukguitars.com/
- Banjo: www.andybanjo.com/terms.htm
- Piano: www.pianos.co.uk/main/how_to_buy.php3
- Clarinet: www.paythepiper.co.uk/clarinet.asp
- Saxophone: www.paythepiper.co.uk/saxophone.asp
- Flute: www.paythepiper.co.uk/flute.asp
- Violin: www.musicaluniverse.com/
- Trumpet: www.paythepiper.co.uk/trumpet.asp
- Drums: www.drumlanduk.com/
- Specialised insurance for musical instruments; free online quotes: www.allianzcornhillmusicalinsurance.co.uk

Performing with your instrument

Bands

- Forming Bands: 2,000 rock and pop groups looking for new members; puts you in contact with players in your part of the country: www.formingbands.co.uk
- African hand drumming: www.drumjam.co.uk.
- West African drum group, contact African Drumbeat: www.african-drumbeat.co.uk
- British Federation of Brass Bands: www.bfbb.co.uk

Folk

- The British Banjo, Mandolin and Guitar Federation lists folk guitar and banjo festivals and other activities: www.banjomandolinguitar.co.uk.
- The English Folk Dance and Song Society: details of traditional folk music groups and activities: www.efdss.org
- Direct Roots: directory of traditional and 'cross-over' or 'fusion' folk music: www.folkarts-england.org

Classical

- Unofficial website giving details for amateur groups around the UK: www.amateurorchestras.org.uk
- Making Music (formerly known as the National Federation of Music Societies), aimed at providing artistic information, training and support services to amateurs: www.makingmusic.org.uk

Index

Acknowledgments

The publishers would like to thank the following for their help with photography: Bush Hall; Guildhall School of Music and Drama; Ben, Harriet and Penny Gunstone; Paul Roberts; Matt Schofield and Trio; The Sky Pirates (Simon Hardeman, Simon Littlefield and Nigel Summerley); Otis Taylor; Gillian Wood.